J. Howard Wert's

GETTYSBURG

A Collection of Relics from the Civil War Battle

Bruce E. Mowday and G. Craig Caba

Schiffer Publishing Ltd

4880 Lower Valley Road • Atglen, PA 19310

Library of Congress Control Number: 2017935083

Designed by Molly Shields
Type set in GoldMine/Times New Roman

ISBN: 978-0-7643-5391-8
Printed in China

Published by Schiffer Publishing, Ltd.
4880 Lower Valley Road
Atglen, PA 19310
Phone: (610) 593-1777; Fax: (610) 593-2002
E-mail: Info@schifferbooks.com
Web: www.schifferbooks.com

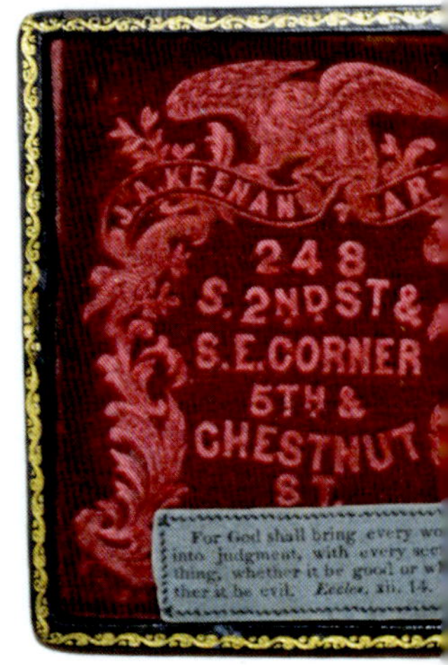

"*Preserve For Prosperity*" – The Wert family motto.

J. Howard Wert's Gettysburg is dedicated to J. Howard Wert, his family, and all those preserving our nation's history.

…Let Virtue Be Your Guide

Colonel Chapman Biddle's relics from Seminary Ridge, July 1, 1863.

CONTENTS

FOREWORD

Just about every element of Gettysburg—the pivotal battle of the Civil War—seems to have been studied and chronicled by historians and those captivated by this critical period of United States history. One person observed in the late 1800s that already too many books had been written about Gettysburg. That person was wrong, as new information is being continuously uncovered. Also, fresh perspectives on Gettysburg the town, Gettysburg the battle, and those connected to Gettysburg are written. Those contributions deserve to be added to the vast library of Gettysburg history.

My involvement in this book, *J. Howard Wert's Gettysburg*, is directly linked to my previous book, *Pickett's Charge: The Untold Story*. I did not set out to write about Gettysburg, but I clearly saw a segment of the battle that had not been totally explored. A number of excellent previous books recounted in detail the Confederate preparation for the attack, those Confederate units taking part in the attack, the execution of the attack, and those to blame for the failure of the charge. What was obviously missing, at least to me, was the story of the Union defenders. Thus, my *Pickett's Charge* tells the story of the Philadelphia Brigade and other brave Union troops that defeated a portion of Gen. Robert E. Lee's army during the afternoon of July 3, 1863. J. Howard called Pickett's Charge the "Grand Assault" as he wrote about his eyewitness account of the Gettysburg battle.

While doing research for *Pickett's Charge* I met Craig Caba through a high school friend, Greg DePedro. Craig owns and does a great job of preserving the famous J. Howard Wert Gettysburg Collection.™ Craig graciously photographed items from the Wert collection for illustrations in *Pickett's Charge*. The photographs greatly enhanced the book, and I received many compliments on the illustrations from the Wert collection. After the book was published, Craig asked if I would be interested in helping him research and write a book on J. Howard Wert, Wert's family, and the Wert collection. Craig said such a book was on his bucket list. I was interested in the project and I answered yes without hesitating. I am so glad I agreed to be part of this project, as I have had a chance to see and touch artifacts from this crucial time in our American history. I also learned a lot about the anti-slavery events that transpired in Gettysburg and Adams County, Pennsylvania, in the years leading up to the Civil War and the battle of Gettysburg.

For me people make history. The dates and outcomes of events are important, but the real story involves the exploits of people, their motivations, their actions, and inactions. For many months I delved into the history of J. Howard and his family. They have a wonderful story to tell. Family members fought in the French and Indian War, the American Revolution, the War of 1812, and the Civil War. Many family members and friends were involved in Underground Railroad activities in the Gettysburg area and throughout Adams County.

The Wert family began collecting historic artifacts long before July 1863. The family has many close connections to the leading founders of this nation, including George Washington. Thaddeus Stevens, a congressman and leading abolitionist, was a close friend of the Wert family. The Wert family preserved an amazing collection over generations, and it was the desire of J. Howard to keep the collection intact. Craig has been true to his wishes.

During these many months of research and writing on J. Howard and his family I have become totally immersed in his world. What a wonderful life he had, starting with his early years as an abolitionist, a student at Pennsylvania—now Gettysburg—College, serving in the Civil War, and working as a newspaper correspondent, educator, and author. One person described J. Howard as a romantic. His Victorian writing style is descriptive, flowing, enthusiastic, and engaging. J. Howard continued his family's tradition of memorializing original eyewitness testimony and historical evidence. In this book Craig and I have attempted to give you the flavor of J. Howard's writing style. The main source of our information has been the writings of J. Howard.

I was especially connected to J. Howard when he wrote about the fighting at the Wheatfield on July 2, 1863, during the battle of Gettysburg. My relative, William Collins, fought with the 61st New York Volunteers there on the second day of the battle and was wounded. J. Howard wrote:

> The writer of his history [Wert] was over the Wheatfield and the adjacent battle line, July 5, 1863, and many subsequent days of that month. No words can portray the awful picture of desolation, devastation and death present. Across the field was the debris of battle, broken muskets, soiled bayonets, shattered ammunition chests, blood defiled clothing, trodden cartridge boxes and splintered swords, rifled knapsacks and battered canteens. Everywhere death, and death in its most abhorrent forms!

J. Howard's vivid description brought forth the horrible experiences endured by my relative and every other soldier on that part of the battlefield. The legacy of J. Howard is the preservation of an important part of our nation's story through his words and the artifacts saved from destruction for future generations. The collection contains important and priceless artifacts from Gettysburg from Northern and Southern participants, and the civilians who experienced the horrors of those three days in July 1863.

J. Howard began his collection of Gettysburg memorabilia by securing discarded military items that were no longer usable by the Union army. As he became known as a collector of Gettysburg artifacts officers, soldiers, politicians, and civilians all gave J. Howard their personal pieces of history. Many were looking for such a person as J. Howard to preserve the Gettysburg legacy.

I hope readers enjoy the story of J. Howard Wert, his family, and their historically significant collection of American artifacts as much as I enjoyed spending time getting to know them. For one who cherishes the artifacts of our nation's history, there is not much better than being able to hold such treasures. I had many wonderful experiences during this research, including touching the saddle of Union Gen. Francis Barlow, who commanded the unit that included my relative. Lt. William Collins must have seen the same saddle. I had a chance to hold in my hands Thaddeus Stevens's walking stick. A replica was used in the movie *Lincoln*. In 2015, the podium used by Pope Francis during his visit to Philadelphia for the World Meeting of Families celebration came from the Wert collection. The same podium was used by President Abraham Lincoln on November 19, 1863, when he gave his famous Gettysburg Address at the dedication of the Soldiers National Cemetery.

The collection has many more items than what are shown and discussed in this book. All Americans have a direct connection to this collection. We hope many people discover this precious link to American history.

Bruce E. Mowday
August 2016

ACKNOWLEDGMENTS

Every book is a product of the contributions of many people. Craig and Bruce thank everyone who took part in the production of this book. Their help is greatly appreciated.

The J. Howard Wert Gettysburg Collection,™ under the stewardship of Craig Caba, provided a vast majority of the information used in this book. Craig greatly aided Bruce's job of researching the material. Craig, the J. Howard Wert expert, also reviewed the manuscript and made many excellent additions.

Thanks go to Cooper Wingert, a young historian and author who toured locations associated with J. Howard Wert along with Craig and Bruce on a cold Friday morning in January 2015. Cooper photographically recorded that tour.

Encouragement was offered all during the book by President Barb Mowery of the Gettysburg Battlefield Preservation Association and her organization. Preservation of historically significant sites and artifacts are championed by Craig and Bruce.

Bruce also did research at the Gettysburg National Military Park and the Adams County Historical Society, as each contain information on the Wert collection. John Heiser, historian at the Division of Interpretation at Gettysburg National Military Park, was of great assistance. He is always a great source, and has aided Bruce in the research of another of his books. Lauren Roedner, archives and collection assistant, and volunteer Roger Heller of the Adams County Historical Society, likewise assisted in the research. During research trips Madeline Butler also provided Bruce with assistance gathering information and asking pertinent questions to focus the research.

Hunter Winters, Eric Gaspich, and Wade Hisero, all young historians, assisted Craig with handling the artifacts and photographing images.

Katherine Harlan is an excellent proofreader and worked her magic on the draft manuscript.

Special thanks goes to everyone at Schiffer Publishing, including publisher Pete Schiffer, who was involved in the project from the beginning. Our editor Catherine Mallette guided us through the editorial process and Schiffer photographer Carey Massimini greatly aided in the shooting of the fine artifacts from the Wert collection. Carey and Doug Congdon-Martin were an immense help setting up the camera and lighting for the photography at Schiffer and very patient when asked numerous times for their expert assistance.

During a number of trips to Schiffer Wert family artifacts had to be transported from the ground floor to the second floor photography studio. The process involved a fork lift and we were glad that John Fedastian and Steve Taylor had the expertise to transport the historic items with skill and care.

We thank everyone who aided in this book.

Relics from General George G. Meade's headquarters.

INTRODUCTION

The oldest collection of Americana from Gettysburg was started by the Wert family. Having its origins in eighteenth century colonial Pennsylvania, this German family saved important heirlooms marking its accomplishments in the new nation. Members of the family actively participated in the French and Indian Wars, the American Revolution, the War of 1812, and the Civil War. During the early days of the War for Independence they marched to Boston to support American forces, and they were present during the British surrender at Yorktown.

Inn owner Dr. Jacob Wert was acquainted with Benjamin Rush, the famed doctor from the American Revolution. Jacob's son, also named Jacob, fought in the Revolution as a foot solider and later became a gentleman farmer and high constable in Adams County. Born in 1787, Adam Wert continued the family's tradition of supporting the young nation. He fought in the War of 1812, was a burgess of Gettysburg, and an educator and enlightened farmer. One of his close friends was Thaddeus Stevens, a prominent statesman who championed the abolition of slavery during the Civil War era.

In 1841, Adam and Catherine Houghtelin Wert had a son, J. Howard Wert, who would later turn the family's collection into one of the premier private collections of history in America. When the Civil War began the Wert family lived three miles south of Gettysburg on their ancestral farm Wolf's Walk, along the Baltimore Pike. The family was known for its Christian convictions. Adam was a staunch temperance man and an energetic abolitionist. Aunt Katie, as Catherine Houghtelin Wert was known, embraced humbleness and generosity. She was also an heir to family wealth. The Wert family greatly influenced the running of the Gettysburg Bank, an influence that aided the abolitionist cause in the early 1860s. J. Howard graduated from Pennsylvania College—now Gettysburg College—in 1861, and was a published author and teacher. He joined the Adams Rifles, a local militia organized to protect Pennsylvania's borders from a Confederate invasion in 1863.

When Gen. Robert E. Lee's army invaded Pennsylvania J. Howard acted as a scout and spy. He was captured and escaped. He made his way to Wolf's Walk and acted as a guide for Gen. George G. Meade during the pivotal battle of Gettysburg. J. Howard's knowledge of his boyhood terrain was vital in placement of troops during the three-day battle. He guided Gen. John Reynolds's First Corps to the seminary and then assisted in the unit's retreat to Cemetery Hill on July 1, 1863. Later he guided troops to Little Round Top, where Gen. James Longstreet's Confederate units were repulsed on July 2, 1863. J. Howard led Gen. John W. Geary's division to Culp's Hill. During the battle Adam Wert, J. Howard's father, shared his maps of Gettysburg at Wolf's Walk with Geary and Gen. Henry Slocum. Adam Wert and members of his family also gave shelter, food, and comfort to wounded soldiers.

Immediately after the battle the Wert family helped Union and Confederate soldiers. Aunt Katie nursed and prayed for many a noble soldier in field hospitals and Camp Letterman, the main Union hospital. J. Howard helped relatives of slain soldiers find the graves of their loved ones. J. Howard also wrote articles for newspapers, recording experiences from the battlefield. During this period Adam Wert encouraged his son, J. Howard, to preserve artifacts from the battle. J. Howard began gathering discarded relics as symbols of military valor and historic mementos. Over time this collecting grew to epic proportions.

Returning from the war, J. Howard went back to teaching, becoming Adams County's superintendent of schools. He also became active in the Grand Army of the Republic (GAR) organization. J. Howard also assisted his friend John Bachelder in publishing a book on the twentieth anniversary of the Battle of Gettysburg. J. Howard's research and interviews with veterans gave him renewed interest in his collections. Fellow Civil War veterans recognized that J. Howard wanted to preserve the artifacts for posterity. Veterans and others connected with Gettysburg gave items to J. Howard, and his fashionable three-story home in Harrisburg became a repository for Gettysburg relics. Many prominent veterans visited the Wert Harrisburg home, including Gen. Dan Sickles, Maj. John Bigelow, and Gen. Charles Graham, who were wounded during the Battle of Gettysburg and were taken prisoner. Sickles was also wounded at Gettysburg at the Trostle farm and lost his leg. Sickles was treated near Wolf's Walk on July 2, 1863, at the Mark-Shaeffer house. The house was across the Baltimore Pike from the Wert farm.

On March 27, 1910, the *New York Herald* wrote:

> Probably the rarest and most valuable private collection of war relics from the battlefields of the Civil War is that owned by Professor J. Howard Wert. Gettysburg was his home and he was there during the great decisive battle, acting as a guide to the Union forces and doing other patriotic work. His Gettysburg relics were gathered after the battle and labeled with inscriptions, showing what part of the field they came from. . . . There are many things that are seldom found in similar collections.

The Wert collection has significant material pertaining to the Underground Railroad and anti-slavery movement in Adams County. Three generations of Wert family members demonstrated against slavery.

J. Howard's collection was kept intact by his son, Howard Houck Wert. The pair made many trips to Gettysburg. J. Howard Wert's 1916 will declared that the collection should be kept intact and not divided. Future generations would be best served by the complete collection. The collection remains virtually intact today.

G. Craig Caba
August 2016

Battle of Gettysburg

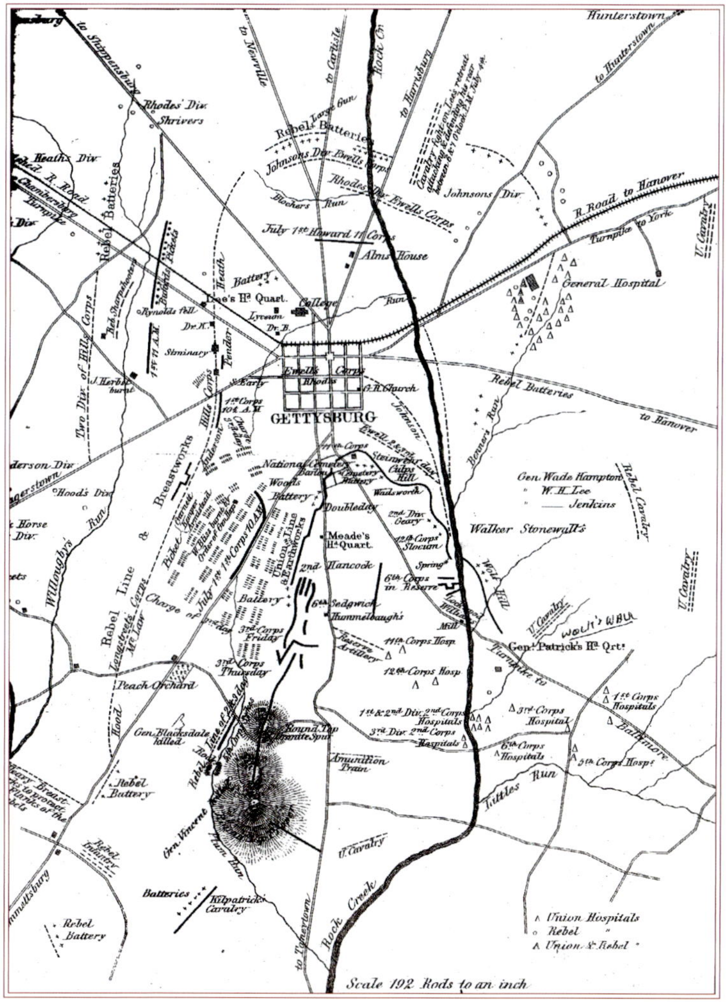

Chapter One

CAPTURED

Panic, fear, and dread paralyzed many a citizen of central Pennsylvania when the Confederate army, under the command of Gen. Robert E. Lee, invaded the Keystone State during late June 1863.

Lee's forces quickly fanned out across the rich farmland of Pennsylvania and occupied towns and villages as far east as the Susquehanna River and north to the outskirts of Harrisburg, Pennsylvania's capital city. Towns were forced by the Southern army to pay ransom or face being put to the torch. Union militia destroyed a bridge over the Susquehanna River by fire at Wrightsville, rather than have the span utilized by the Southern army to march on Lancaster—a key manufacturing center—and Philadelphia. Crops and other material essential to the operation and sustainability of the Confederate army were confiscated from residents of Pennsylvania. The whole Cumberland Valley of Pennsylvania was invaded from Carlisle to the Mason-Dixon line.

Pennsylvania was under siege, and residents of the commonwealth rallied to defend their native land. One such defender was young J. Howard Wert, a member of the militia unit Adams Rifles. J. Howard was a Gettysburg resident and an 1861 graduate of Pennsylvania College. Members of Wert's family had fought for the nation in previous conflicts, including the French and Indian Wars, American Revolution, and the War of 1812. J. Howard was carrying on the family tradition of defending America's freedoms.

Wert family members were staunch opponents of anti-slavery and well-known in the Gettysburg area for their views on the subject. J. Howard's prewar anti-slavery activities put him in double jeopardy, as he acted as a scout north of Gettysburg, in the vicinity of Harrisburg, in the days preceding the battle of Gettysburg.

Besides being a Union scout, J. Howard was carrying—concealed in the lining of his hat—a special pass from the War Department in Washington, DC, under the authority of Secretary of War Edwin Stanton. On June 16, 1863, Assistant Adjutant Gen. C. W. Foster signed the pass.

The pass was issued in connection with J. Howard being considered an officer in a regiment yet to be recruited of African-American soldiers. Plans had been formed for such a unit in May 1863. If captured and the pass was discovered, J. Howard would be subjected to harsh treatment by his Confederate foes. A likely punishment would have been death.

Members of the Wert family were great friends with Thaddeus Stevens, a congressman from Pennsylvania who had lived in Gettysburg, served on the Gettysburg Council with Adam Wert, and was active in anti-slavery activities, including the Underground Railroad. Stevens was the person who urged J. Howard to go to Washington to seek service as an officer in the proposed African-American military unit. Stevens also used his influence so J. Howard could secure an interview in the War Department.

The Confederate invasion of Pennsylvania curtailed J. Howard's efforts to recruit African-Americans for the United States army. Defeating Confederate Gen. Robert E. Lee's army and driving the

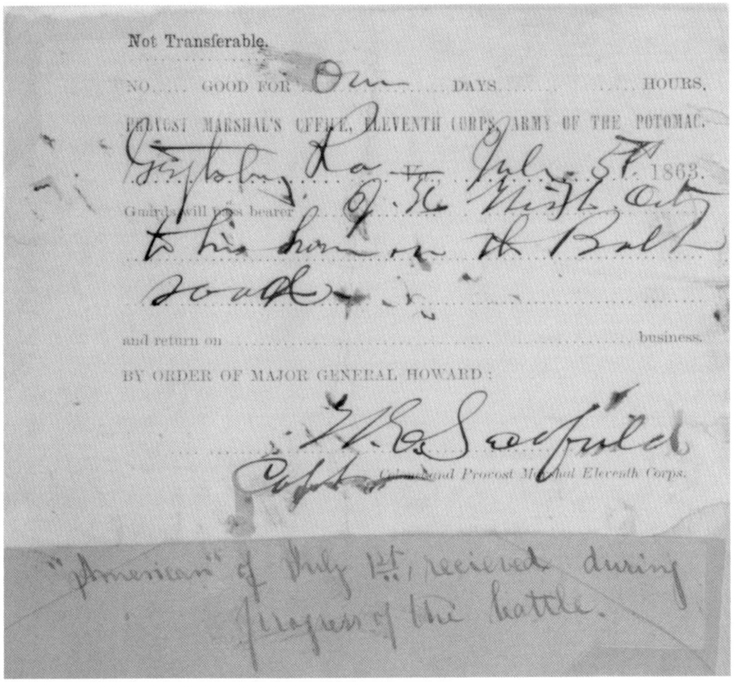
Not Transferable.

NO..... GOOD FOR One DAYS..... HOURS.

PROVOST MARSHAL'S OFFICE, ELEVENTH CORPS, ARMY OF THE POTOMAC.

Gettysburg Pa July 5th 1863.

Guards will pass bearer J. H. Wert Citz to his home on the Balt road.

and return on ..... business.

BY ORDER OF MAJOR GENERAL HOWARD:

[signature] Capt ... and Provost Marshal Eleventh Corps.

"American" of July 1st, recieved during progress of the battle.

Pass issued by Gen. Oliver O. Howard's Union 11th Corps on July 1, 1863, that allowed (commissioned) J. Howard Wert to travel within Union lines and guide troops. The pass was good until July 5. Note the hurried writing due to the action of battle.

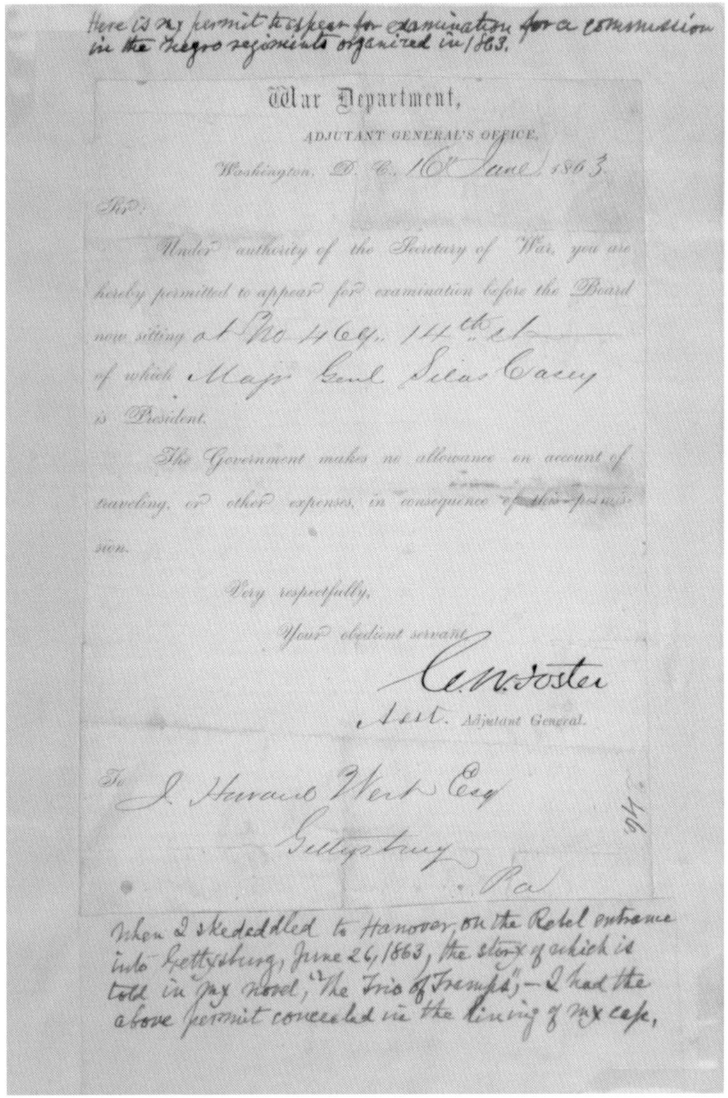
Here is my permit to appear for examination for a commission in the negro regiments organized in 1863.

War Department,

ADJUTANT GENERAL'S OFFICE,

Washington, D. C., 16th June 1863.

Sir:

Under authority of the Secretary of War, you are hereby permitted to appear for examination before the Board now sitting at No 469. 14th st of which Major Genl Silas Casey is President.

The Government makes no allowance on account of traveling, or other expenses, in consequence of this permission.

Very respectfully,

Your obedient servant,

C. W. Foster

Asst. Adjutant General.

To J. Howard Wert Esq
Gettysburg
Pa

When I skedaddled to Hanover, on the Rebel entrance into Gettysburg, June 26, 1863, the story of which is told in my novel, "The Trio of Tramps," — I had the above permit concealed in the lining of my cap.

Pass carried by J. Howard Wert in his cap during the Battle of Gettysburg.

invading army from his homeland was the only major focus of J. Howard and his neighbors during the early summer weeks of 1863.

Returning to Gettysburg in the days preceding the battle, J. Howard volunteered his services as a special scout under the command of Maj. Granville Haller. Haller, of the 7th US Infantry, had been ordered by Union Maj. Gen. Darius Couch to recruit Gettysburg area citizens to fight the Confederates. Haller made his headquarters in the old Eagle Hotel in Gettysburg and directed two cavalry units as the invasion developed. J. Howard's knowledge of the area was invaluable to the Union army. He knew many of the little-used byways of the area from his college days helping escaped slaves navigate the Underground Railroad.

J. Howard borrowed his father's blind horse and wagon to begin a scouting mission designed to identify the whereabouts and the number of Confederate troops in the area. Dressed as a farmer, he headed toward the Confederate army. His dress made J. Howard a spy rather than an army scout. Near Fayetteville, Pennsylvania, J. Howard was detained by Confederate forces under the command of Gen. Richard Ewell. While being held in custody he saw Confederate Gen. Robert E. Lee near his tent. J. Howard recalled that Lee was dressed in common soldier's garb and wore no signs of his rank.

J. Howard was detained because of a Confederate soldier who had once lived in Gettysburg. The rebel soldier knew of Adam Wert's abolitionist sympathies. The soldier believed J. Howard was more than a mere farmer and reported his suspicion to Confederate officers. J. Howard was detained, then was forced to march with the Confederate army towards Carlisle. As the Rebel army prepared to seize the town just west of Harrisburg it was recalled to Gettysburg to rejoin the rest of Lee's army. J. Howard took advantage of the confusion of the moment to escape and made his way to Perry County, where he encountered Union troops and gave a detailed account of the Confederate forces he saw under Ewell's command.

As the scattered corps of the Confederate army converged on Gettysburg, J. Howard was ordered to return to his hometown. Using the knowledge of the land between Perry County and Gettysburg he learned during his days working the Underground Railroad J. Howard was able to evade Confederate forces. At the William and Phoebe Wright family farm near York Springs, in Adams County, J. Howard secured a fresh horse from his Quaker friends. At the Wright's farm J. Howard also received the latest news of Confederate movements around Gettysburg. The Wright farm was a former stop on the Underground Railroad and just fifteen miles from Gettysburg.

As for Ewell and his men, they were near Carlisle on June 28, and threatening Harrisburg when Lee summoned them to Gettysburg to face the United States Army of the Potomac under their new commander, Gen. George G. Meade.

Arriving at his Gettysburg home Wolf's Walk in the morning hours of July 1, J. Howard immediately went to work without resting. After Adam Wert updated J. Howard on the latest news J. Howard proceeded directly to Gettysburg. He traveled across then tranquil farm fields to the seminary south and west of the town's business district. During the next seventy-two hours those same fields would erupt into chaos and become the final resting place of many brave Americans. J. Howard volunteered to guide the First Corps as the unit, under the command of Pennsylvania Gen. John Reynolds, approached Gettysburg. Knowing shortcuts through the area, J. Howard led Reynolds's men to support Gen. John Buford's cavalry just west of Seminary Ridge. Buford had held off a larger Confederate force during the morning hours in an effort to secure the high ground at Gettysburg, a key defensive position which resulted in ultimate Union victory. Reynolds deployed his troops along Willoughby Run. Not long after reaching the field Reynolds was killed by a Confederate sharpshooter sometime between 10:00 and 11:00 a.m.

Later in the morning J. Howard aided Gen. Oliver O. Howard upon his arrival on the field and directed the 11th Corps north of Pennsylvania College, where J. Howard had recently graduated. A portion of the battle was raging in the area from Oak Ridge to Harrisburg Pike.

J. Howard had no time to rest. Early in the afternoon, during a lull in the battle, he was sent about five miles south of Gettysburg to a little settlement known as Two Taverns, about a mile south of Wolf's Walk. J. Howard was instructed to assist in the direction of Gen. Henry Slocum, the right wing commander of the Union army, to the battlefield.

Slocum arrived at Two Taverns the morning of July 1, but did not proceed to Gettysburg, despite orders from Gen. Howard and reports of gunfire: a clear indication that a battle was starting. After receiving additional orders in mid-afternoon and with J. Howard's assistance Slocum advanced. J. Howard guided the 12th Corps across White's Run Road to the Hanover Road, where the Union men challenged Confederate Gen. Ewell's troops for control of Wolf and Culp's hills.

Slocum arrived at Gettysburg about 6:00 p.m. and took over command of the Union forces until Meade arrived about midnight.

Wolf's Walk became an important piece of the Union defense at Gettysburg. Five generals, including Slocum and John Geary, visited Wolf's Walk to view a large wall map of Adams County owned by Adam Wert. Wert family members were active treating wounded soldiers during the fighting. Wert's mother Catherine Houghtelin Wert tended to Gen. Thomas Kane at their home. Kane was suffering from pneumonia at the time of the battle. Nearby Baltimore Pike was also one of the main roads used by the Union army for deployment of arriving troops and transportation of supplies.

The original Wolf's Walk farm consisted of more than 200 acres authorized from a land grant from William Penn. The property was first surveyed in 1763. On the original parcel was the farm of Daniel Sheaffer, a former congressman. The Sheaffer house was built about 1780, and is said to be the first brick house in Adams County. For a time the house operated as a tavern under a sign of George Washington. During Gettysburg the house served as a field hospital and was the location Union Gen. Daniel Sickles had his leg amputated after being wounded by a projectile on the second day of fighting. Sickles stayed overnight at the farm house before being transported to Washington, DC. Sheaffer offered hospitality to Sickles, who was also a former congressman. Sickles recalled, "In a moment I was removed from the ground to the field hospital on the Baltimore Pike that night, in the gloaming, Dr. Calhoun cut off the useless limb." J. Howard wrote that he, "saw the noble chieftain borne with shattered leg to the somber brick house on the Baltimore Pike, at that time occupied by Daniel Sheaffer."

July 2, 1863, the second day of the battle, was a long and busy one for J. Howard. When the Union's extreme left was in danger of being flanked he piloted troops to the endangered Round Tops portion of the field. J. Howard was with Col. Strong Vincent just before Vincent died leading the life-and-death defense of Little Round Top. If Little Round Top had fallen to Confederate forces Gettysburg would have been a Southern victory.

J. Howard secured his first Gettysburg battlefield artifact that afternoon, picking up a piece of the shell that nearly wounded him. J. Howard recalled the iron fragment was still warm when he handled the projectile. That day J. Howard traversed the entire Union line from Round Tops to Culp's Hill. The Union defensive line was in the form of a fish hook. During the late evening hours he led part of Gen. John Geary's division from the area of the Round Tops back to the army's right flank at Culp's Hill.

While not confirmed, reports have J. Howard being present at Meade's headquarters at the Lydia Leister farm on Taneytown Road late in the evening of July 2. Meade held an important meeting with his generals on the strategy to be employed on July 3, the final and deciding day of the Gettysburg battle.

Union Gen. Geary's troops and others of the 12th Corps at Culp's Hill fought off the Confederate assault the morning of July 3. In the afternoon J. Howard was again doing vital work for Meade's army, as he led reinforcements to help stop the famed Pickett's Charge. J. Howard called the action the "Grand Assault."

In the coming years J. Howard used his eyewitness experiences at Gettysburg to write a number of detailed newspaper articles, pamphlets, and books on the battle, and also on individuals, both military and civilian, affected by the fight.

Chapter Two

WERT FAMILY

The Wert family came to Pennsylvania in the eighteenth century from Germany. America quickly became the adopted home of the Wert family, and family members were quick to take up arms in its defense when threatened.

Jacob Wert, known in family records as Jacob Wert the elder because his son carried the same name, came to Adams County, Pennsylvania, from Whitehall, Northampton County, Pennsylvania, in 1786. As a teenager Jacob was recruited by Benjamin Franklin to take part in the French and Indian War. Jacob the elder was a wagoneer during British Gen. Edward Braddock's march in July 1755 to western Pennsylvania. George Washington, then twenty-three and a colonel, was an aide-de-camp to Braddock during the campaign, which ended in defeat for the British and the death of Braddock.

Jacob was well educated. He was fluent in German and English and diligently studied the Bible. He became a successful farmer and was proficient in medicine and mathematics. Jacob was also a teacher during the winter months when agricultural duties were less demanding. He passed along his knowledge to his neighbors by teaching reading, writing, and mathematics. He also served the community by being appointed to a government post of high constable.

During the American Revolution Jacob volunteered to use his medical knowledge to help American troops. His rank was captain. Jacob became acquainted with Dr. Benjamin Rush. Rush signed the Declaration of Independence and was surgeon general of the Continental army. Rush taught at the University of Pennsylvania and was the founder of Dickinson College in Carlisle. Rush was also known as a politician, social reformer, teacher, humanitarian, and a supporter of temperance. He also staunchly opposed slavery.

After the American Revolution Jacob purchased a farm west of Hunterstown, on a then major road from York to the Cumberland Valley near the Conewago Church. On the property Jacob practiced medicine, ran a tavern, and also farmed. Rush became a frequent visitor to the Wert home. Rush stopped at the Wert property on his way to Dickinson College. Jacob recorded subjects they discussed, including medicine, temperance, and slavery. Rush and Franklin were early members of the Pennsylvania Abolition Society, with Franklin serving as an early president of the organization.

President George Washington was a visitor at the Wert Tavern in July 1794. Local masons, according to Wert family records, greeted Washington as he made his way to the Wert Tavern. Washington joined the army he sent to Western Pennsylvania to put down a protest against taxes. Washington's visit at the Wert Tavern took place after Washington departed Carlisle after the tax revolt, known as the Whiskey Rebellion, had been suppressed.

The tavern was a meeting place for local Free Masons and veterans of the American Revolution. Many of the local veterans were at Valley Forge for the harsh winter of 1777–1778. The German speaking residents acted as translators for Gen. Friedrich Wilhelm von Steuben, who trained American soldiers and helped to turn the civilian fighting force into a professional army that would defeat the highly respected British army.

Members of the Wert family participated in the quest for liberty of all men from the French and Indian War through the Civil War. Rooted in holy scripture and the principles stated in the Declaration of Independence, the Wert family formed its staunch political philosophy to oppose the evils of slavery and support liberty for all. Respect and responsibility were cherished virtues in the Wert family.

One of Jacob's sons, known as Jacob the younger, was a youthful soldier in the American Revolution and later became a gentleman farmer. He was born in 1758. Jacob the younger was involved in finance, and was elected high constable in Adams County. In 1797, Adam Wert was born to Jacob and Eva Mark Wert. The family lived on a portion of Eva Mark Wert's ancestral farm Wolf's Walk. The farm is about three miles south of Gettysburg along the Baltimore Pike. Eva Wert was born on November 8, 1771, and died on August 13, 1853.

Adam was privately schooled and learned English and German. Adam continued the family tradition of community service. He served in the War of 1812. He marched with a local militia company to the defense of Baltimore during the British invasion. After the British threat subsided Adam returned to Adams County to farm. As his grandfather had, during the winter months Adam taught neighbors, especially rural children. Adam believed education was critical to a healthy and knowledgeable citizenry. An educated public ensured a healthy democracy, Adam believed. Education and teaching became family vocations.

Another distant family member was William Wirt. (Some members of the family spell the last name Wirt instead of Wert.) Wirt gained national fame for his work in the unsuccessful prosecution of Aaron Burr—the third vice president of the United States—for treason. In 1807, President Thomas Jefferson asked Wirt to be the prosecutor in the Burr trial. Wirt delivered a four-hour speech during the trial that was hailed for its eloquent appeal, polished wit, and logical reasoning. Wirt was appointed United States attorney general by President James Monroe. He held the position for twelve years, the longest tenure of anyone holding the office.

Wirt met Jefferson and Monroe while living in Charlottesville, Virginia. Wirt was an unsuccessful presidential candidate in 1832. In 1817, Wirt authored *Sketches of the Life and Character of Patrick Henry*. The book was published in Philadelphia by James Webster. Wirt never met Henry, but did receive information from those who knew Henry, including Jefferson. Wirt wrote:

> Mr. Jefferson too, has exercised his well-known kindness and candor on this occasion; having not only favored the author with a very full communication in the first instance; but assisted him, subsequently and repeatedly, with his able counsel, in reconciling apparent contradictions, and clearing away difficulties of fact.

In the 1880s, J. Howard enjoyed a warm relationship with Patrick Henry's grandson, Col. William Aylette of Gen. George Pickett's Division. Aylette was wounded as the famous Pickett's Charge began on the third day of the battle of Gettysburg.

Adam Wert was also a burgess of Gettysburg. His close friend was Thaddeus Stevens, who lived for a period of time in Gettysburg and was a town official along with Adam. Stevens, an attorney from New England, shared many of the same beliefs as the Wert family. The two men served together on the Gettysburg town council in 1831. Jacob was a great supporter of Stevens, especially early in Stevens's career.

In 1833, Stevens was elected to the state house of representatives representing Adams County and served until 1839. He later moved to Lancaster and was elected to Congress.

After the death of his father Adam possessed a considerable estate. He married Catherine Houghtelin and the couple lived on Wolf's Walk. Catherine was heir to a substantial family fortune.

The Houghtelin family also actively participated in the American Revolution, as members marched to Boston early in the war and spent Winter 1777–1778 at Valley Forge and Pennypacker Mills outside Philadelphia. Capt. Wilhelm Houghtelin was a member of the Pennsylvania Flying Camp and served under Gen. George Washington and the Marquis de Lafayette.

On February 12, 1841, J. Howard was born to Adam and Catherine Houghtelin Wert. Around the community the family was also known for their Christian conviction and good deeds. Catherine, known to many as Aunt Katie, was characterized as humble and generous. Adam, like his father, was active raising money for churches through lotteries. Adam also sold turnpike stock and speculated in real estate, owning a number of income producing properties.

The Wert family was influential in the community, especially with Gettysburg Bank. That influence would be used to great effect to oppose slavery in the coming years. The bank was known to threaten to revoke mortgages of those cooperating with slave hunters unless that cooperation ceased.

Wert family members were strong supporters of the Whig political party. Whig leaders included Daniel Webster, Henry Clay, William Henry Harrison, Zachary Taylor, and Winfield Scott. The Whig Party disbanded as the Civil War was about to begin and many, including the Wert family, joined the new Republican Party, soon to be spearheaded by Abraham Lincoln.

J. Howard grew up being told family stories about the American Revolution and the War of 1812. He entered Gettysburg High School in 1853, and three years later he was ready to begin his education at Pennsylvania College. He graduated with honors in 1861, the opening year of the American Civil War. J. Howard's first teaching job upon completion of college was in York Springs, a Quaker community active in anti-slavery activity.

Adam wrote about his philosophy on slavery and some of his letters were printed in Boston publications. J. Howard also served for the Union during the Civil War. An artifact in the Wert collection dated August 9, 1862, indicates J. Howard was paid for his thirty days of service with Adams County as a volunteer. He was with his militia just after the battle of Antietam.

Wert Family Images and Artifacts

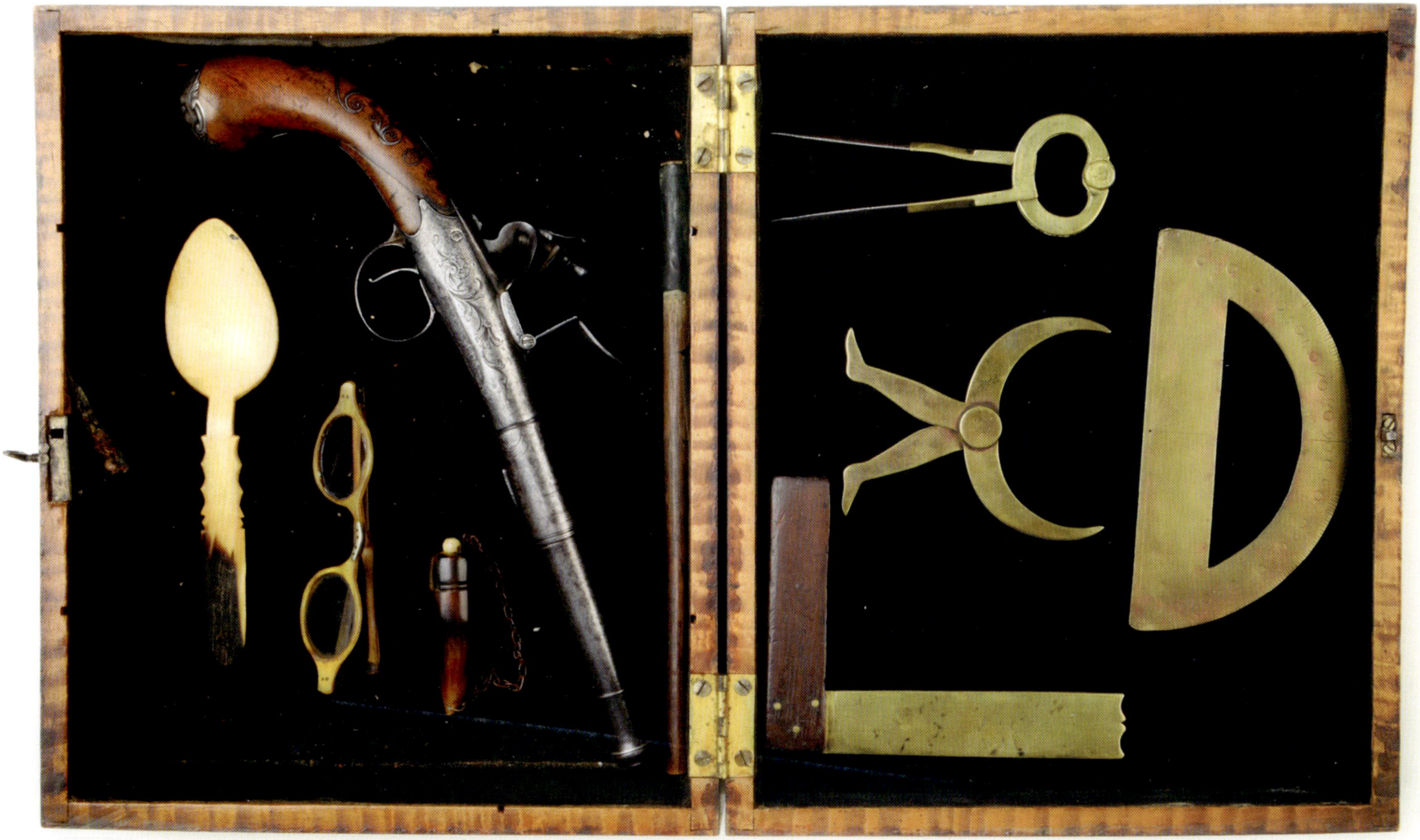

Capt. Wilhelm Houghtelin's eighteenth-century memento box containing surveying instruments, horn spoon, horn glasses, salt container, and silver-mounted pistol.

Capt. Wilhelm Houghtelin's Pennsylvania Continental currency, leather wallet, hand-embroidered coin purse, and coins. The captain was a member of the 7th Pennsylvania Regiment and among the troops who marched to assist the Minute Men of Massachusetts at the start of the revolution.

Wert's maternal grandfather Capt. Wilhelm Houghtelin's American Revolution sword. Of Dutch ancestry, the Houghtelins were early settlers in Adams County before the war.

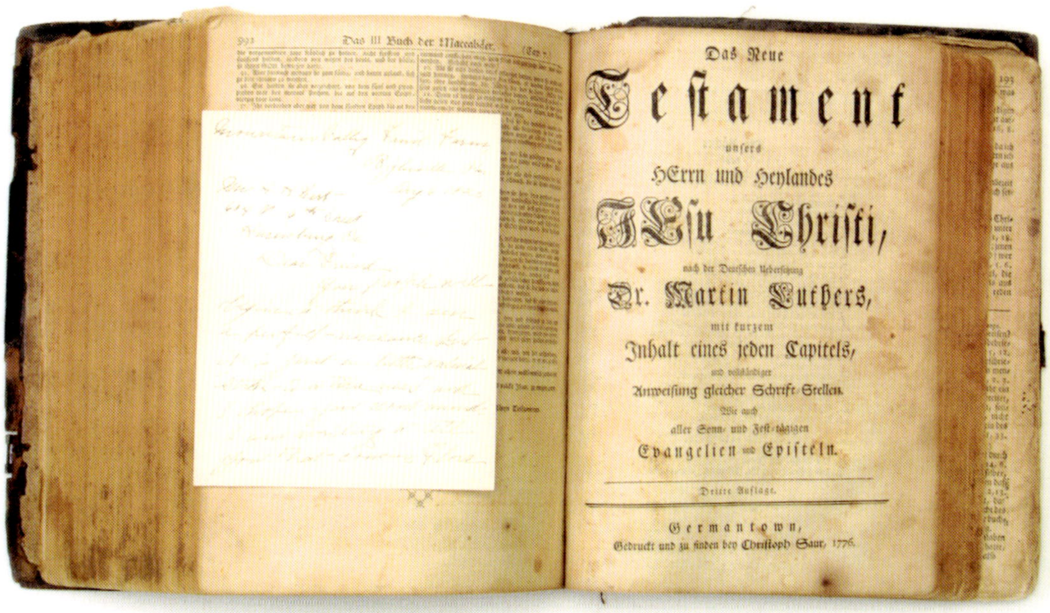

The Wert family German Bible by Christopher Sauer made in 1776. The Werts' knowledge of German was later used by Baron von Steuban to help translate military drills into English at Valley Forge.

Captain Dr. Jacob Wert's snuff or pill box. The inscription reflects his Revolutionary War sentiments.

Congressman Thaddeus Stevens' portable desk with artifacts.

Congressman Thaddeus Stevens' patriotic Eagle walking stick carried as a congressman.

President George Washington's official documents box used in Philadelphia. The box was given to Jacob Wert by Benjamin Rush, who stopped at his inn on his journey to Carlisle and Dickinson College. A gold leaf presidential eagle dominates the interior.

Blown Stiegel glass made in the late eighteenth century painted with George Washington upon his horse. The glass was owned by Capt. Jacob Wert and used at the inn. According to family tradition, the captain toasted Washington with other local Masons upon his return from the Whiskey Rebellion.

Adam Wert's War of 1812 veteran's badge and red leather wallet.

Folk art portrait on a wooden board of Capt. Wilhelm Houghtelin by Adam Wert.

Chapter Three

GETTYSBURG ABOLITIONISTS

The Wert family was among the first in Adams County to openly oppose slavery. Family members became active in the anti-slavery movement and later the Underground Railroad, and aided family friend Congressman Thaddeus Stevens in his fight to end the practice of slavery throughout the United States.

Not every resident of Adams County supported the anti-slavery movement. Adams County shares the Mason-Dixon Line with Maryland, then a slave-holding state. Gettysburg, the Adams County seat of government, is a scant six miles from the Maryland line. Some of the wagon and carriage production in the county was sold in southern states. Slaves were also owned by prominent Adams County residents in the early part of the nineteenth century, including James McSherry, who served in Congress and the Pennsylvania legislature, and fought in the War of 1812. The McPherson family owned slaves in the late 1700s, and a grandson, Edward McPherson, was later a congressman from Gettysburg, and then chief clerk of the House of Representatives. He was an abolitionist and recorded anti-slavery votes for the 13th Amendment on January 31, 1865. The 13th Amendment abolished slavery and involuntary servitude.

Adams County was formed in January 1800 and named for President John Adams; previously it was part of York County. Gettysburg was an excellent selection for the seat of county government, as the town was linked by various roads to Baltimore, Harrisburg, Chambersburg, York, Lancaster, and other thriving towns and cities. Several turnpikes were also constructed with links to Gettysburg. The vast road system led to Gettysburg playing an important role in the Underground Railroad. The road system was also one of the reasons the battle of Gettysburg was fought.

By the 1830s, some members of the Gettysburg community were quietly meeting to discuss ways to oppose slavery. At a Fourth of July picnic in 1836 at McAllister's Mill, along Rock Creek, just south of Gettysburg, the abolition movement in Adams County formally organized. James McAllister presided over the meeting and Adam Wert, McAllister's neighbor, was appointed secretary. Formal resolutions were adopted opposing slavery. A newspaper article and editorial was printed a week later in Gettysburg's *The Star & Republican Banner*. Publisher Robert Middleton's editorial noted the patriotic spirit of the group and supported, "liberty of speech and the right of free discussion."

On September 17, 1836 (Constitution Day), the organization held another meeting at Two Taverns, a small village just south of the Wert family farm. Robert Young presided over the meeting and additional detailed resolutions were adopted. The organization stated slavery was totally irreconcilable with the Declaration of Independence. The organization formed a political committee of correspondence to be active in upcoming Congressional elections.

Civic leader Adam Wert—teacher, farmer, and Gettysburg town burgess—became active in the movement, along with his wife Catherine. Catherine was influential in her own right, as she held 2,000 shares of Gettysburg Bank stock in her name, the only woman to possess such a holding. Adam Wert worked in the background of the organization, according to his son J. Howard. "He manipulated the hidden springs, set up the machinery of the meetings, and endeavored to escape the appearance of undue prominence," J. Howard wrote about his father. Adam Wert spent many hours setting up the meetings of the anti-slavery group. A key advisor to Adam Wert was Thaddeus Stevens, a Vermont lawyer who lived in Gettysburg and a political and social friend of the Wert family.

The fledgling abolitionist movement ran into opposition on December 3, 1836, when a meeting was called at the county courthouse in Gettysburg to elect representatives to attend the Pennsylvania Anti-Slavery Convention to be held in Harrisburg on December 19. Citizens with pro-Southern views took over control of the meeting and a resolution was approved saying it was improper to take any further steps to petition Congress to abolish slavery.

J. Howard wrote, "Gettysburg at that time had some young lawyers of violent pro-slavery proclivities. There were business and professional animosities then as violent and vindictive as those in larger cities and of later times." J. Howard wrote that one of the prime businesses in Gettysburg was the construction of carriages sold in the South. The pro-slavery faction did not want to hurt the town's commerce.

After the December 3 meeting the abolitionists attempted to gather in a quiet setting, but the pro-Southern contingent heckled the abolitionists and threw eggs at them, and a fight broke out in the town square. Finally the abolitionists withdrew to the Gettysburg Academy and then to Col. Michael Clarkson's home. The group vowed to continue opposing slavery. Minutes were taken of the meeting and recorded in a book that is part of the Wert collection. Adam Wert and eighteen other residents were reported to be at the meeting.

The Pennsylvania Anti-Slavery Convention was eventually held on January 14, 1837, in Harrisburg. Adam Wert and a number of members of the Gettysburg group attended. John Greenleaf Whittier was also a participant at the convention. Wert and Whittier became friends. The Anti-Slavery Society disbanded three years later in 1840.

On April 17, 1837, Jonathan Blanchard delivered an anti-slavery speech at the courthouse in Gettysburg. Blanchard was one of a number of speakers sent by the American Anti-Slavery Society throughout the country. Blanchard was born in Vermont, received his education at Middlebury College, and was a pastor at the Sixth Presbyterian Church in Cincinnati.

Blanchard's topic was, "Will the agitation of the Abolition Question cause a dissolution of the Union?" Twenty-six years after Blanchard delivered the talk Union and Confederate armies fought at Gettysburg on the dissolution issue. Blanchard answered questions and debated some pro-slavery residents. Then some in the audience voted for a resolution that intimated Blanchard was not welcome in the area.

Wert family friend Stevens was at the next scheduled meeting at the courthouse and spoke in a calm and deliberate manner, according to J. Howard. An open and free discussion of ideas followed and Blanchard completed his talk on slavery and disunion.

The Star and Republican Banner, the Gettysburg newspaper, reported on Blanchard's speech and other anti-slavery issues in the years leading up to the Civil War.

Sons of the Adams County anti-slavery group prominently served during the Civil War. William Wright's son became a general, supervising military railroads. James McAllister's sons all served. John McAllister was a member of the 87th Pennsylvania Volunteers. Samuel and Calvin McAllister rode with the 21st Pennsylvania Cavalry. Theodore McAllister served in Cole's Cavalry, a Maryland Union unit, and was captured and survived Andersonville Prison. James McAllister died at Vicksburg. Samuel Young fought with the First Pennsylvania Reserves at Gettysburg. J. Howard Wert was a special scout for Gen. Meade at Gettysburg and was a member of the 209th Pennsylvania, serving at Petersburg and other engagements.

J. Howard was very active in Gettysburg's Underground Railroad. The basic overland route from Baltimore or Washington for escaped slaves was to Westminster, Maryland. Then the escaped slaves would be taken to the Baltimore Pike to travel on to Gettysburg. From Gettysburg escaped slaves would be helped to continue their northern trek. Adam Wert and James McAllister both lived just south of town on the escape route. Many of the runaways stayed in area barns, natural hiding places, or at McAllister's Mill.

J. Howard wrote about the ruins of McAllister's Mill. The old stone grist mill was erected in 1790 on the banks of Rock Creek close to Baltimore Pike. James McAllister purchased the mill in 1827. "Secluded among the rocks and huge boulders," J. Howard wrote:

> the stone mill was a natural haven for serious work on what will become known as the "Underground Railroad." The stone mill was used as a safe house for fugitive slaves. Once a slave reached the mill his safety was assured. One of the favorite places to conceal fugitive slaves was in the cog pit of the old mill. This room was capable of secreting up to ten slaves. It had a heavy door elevated by an overhead pulley and was concealed by the mill's interior water wheel.

According to J. Howard search parties were unable to find runaway slaves on the property. Also, opposite of the mill was a thickly wooded hill and on the eastern slope was a rocky cavern called Wind Cave. Escaping slaves would at times hide in the cave or the forest. On December 2, 1904, S. R. McAllister wrote a letter saying one of the escaped slaves was a daughter of Confederate Gen. Robert Toombs of Georgia. She eventually made her way to Canada, according to McAllister. She was brought to Wolf's Hill by William Chaplin.

J. Howard also wrote about Chaplin, an active agent of the Underground Railroad from New York. J. Howard estimated Chaplin brought about twenty slaves to Wolf's Hill. Chaplin's final successful trip included a family of four. Slave catchers determined the family must have had help from Chaplin, and on his next mission he was captured in Montgomery County, Maryland. Chaplin was wounded and his carriage riddled with bullets during the encounter with the slave catchers.

James McAllister wrote that some slave hunters from Adams County ended up serving in the Confederate army. J. Howard noted that one African-American man from Gettysburg made a lot of money turning in runaway slaves to slave hunters. During the Battle of Gettysburg McAllister's Mill would be used as a hospital, and would also mark the extreme right flank of the Union line.

Slaves escaping from Virginia and the Cumberland Valley made their way to Hiram Wert's home on Stevens's Caledonia Iron Works in Quincy, Franklin County. From there they walked to Peter Marks's Cashtown Inn. Marks was a cousin of Adam Wert.

Unlike most places, Gettysburg's Underground Railroad involved a real railroad below ground level. Nearby the Cashtown Inn was an unfinished railroad project championed by Stevens and known locally as the Tapeworm Railroad, because all of the planned switchbacks looked like a tapeworm. Escaped slaves at

Cashtown were told to follow the unfinished railroad toward Gettysburg. The railroad bed ended at Stevens's home, near Pennsylvania College. The unfinished railroad was below grade, and thus underground. The house Stevens owned was later known as the Thompson house, Confederate Gen. Robert E. Lee's headquarters during the battle of Gettysburg.

Frequently the slaves were met by John "Jack" Hopkins, a black custodian of Pennsylvania College. The college was at the end of the unfinished railroad. If Hopkins was not here the fugitives were told to go to the stone house on the left, which was owned by Stevens and rented to the Thompson family. Hopkins kept a stack of firewood and slaves were told to hide there if Hopkins was not around. If not contacted in a reasonable amount of time the slaves were told to retrace their steps to the Thompson house. The Thompsons provided food, water, and other assistance. From Gettysburg, the escaped slaves would be taken to Quakers in the York Springs area and then to Harrisburg.

Escaped slaves were sometimes directed east toward York, Columbia, Lancaster, and Philadelphia. Gettysburg was not considered a safe place for slaves to end their escape from the South because of the pro-slavery support of some of the populace and closeness to the Mason-Dixon Line.

J. Howard wrote about one instance when he was nine years old. He helped his father assist in an escape. The year was 1849. This was J. Howard's first experience aiding an escaped slave. J. Howard recalled a chill, damp, cloudy evening when he saw his father arrive by carriage with an escaped slave acting as his coachman. Slave hunters were in close pursuit and J. Howard was enlisted as a guide to take the slave to Wolf's Hill by back paths. Adam Wert told his son that the hunters were too close to stay to the main road (Baltimore Pike). J. Howard related seeing the pursuing hunters less than half a mile from their location.

Taking a seat next to the slave, J. Howard guided him along the unmarked path. The trio drove through mud that reached halfway up the hub of the carriage's wheel. J. Howard urged the slave to drive faster as they went down a hill. "Better git down to it faster than that if you want to git away," J. Howard recalled saying. He then guided the slave through woods on a ridge that ran parallel with the road. The pursuers did not give up their chase, and at one point were only 200 yards away from J. Howard and the slave.

At that point J. Howard took over driving the carriage, telling the slave he "couldn't drive fur nithin." J. Howard drove the coach over and through water, stumps, and gnarled and protruding roots of giant trees, at times barely squeezing between the barriers. The boy kept up the harrowing trek until reaching a labyrinth of trees and rocks, where he stopped at the base of a bluff. J. Howard was sure the pursing party could not have kept up with his pace. He went to seek help from James McAllister. One of McAllister's sons helped hide the slave in a rock cave deep in a dense thicket of scrubby pine bushes.

J. Howard was correct about the pursing slave catchers. After the chase the wreckage of their carriage was found. The slave hunters continued on foot, and at one point passed within yards of the secreted slave and members of the Wert and McAllister clans without seeing them. Two nights later the slave made his way to Harrisburg.

Area abolitionists were also involved in aiding the escape of some of John Brown's raiders, according to a letter written by Alexander K. McClure to J. Howard on December 10, 1904. Brown led a raid on the federal arsenal at Harpers Ferry—then Virginia—in 1859. Brown attempted to start a slave rebellion, but the raid failed and a majority of his twenty-man force was either killed or later executed.

McClure, who was listed as prothonotary of the Supreme Court of Pennsylvania on the letterhead, wrote to J. Howard asking for information on the Underground Railroad. McClure, besides being an attorney, editor, and politician, authored history books in his later years.

McClure referenced an article J. Howard wrote mentioning Dr. William Rutherford, who helped slaves escape and hid them on his family farm in Paxtang, Pennsylvania, near Harrisburg.

McClure wrote:

> I remember that we sent John Brown's son and two or three others of John Brown's party that escaped from Harpers Ferry severely wounded from Chambersburg over the mountains to Bella Mills, where they were met by some person under the direction of Dr. Rutherford of Harrisburg, and he planned the scheme with us to have them escape. We had them in Chambersburg for two or three days and nights, as they were unable to travel, and fed them in the forest where they were hidden.

Seven conspirators escaped, including Brown's son Owen. Two were soon captured and executed. Owen Brown, Francis Meriam, Charles Tidd, Barclay Coppoc, and Osborn Anderson were never captured.

McClure lived in Chambersburg at the time of the Civil War, and his home was deliberately burned to the ground during a Confederate raid on the town in 1864.

In the years preceding the Civil War J. Howard was a student at Pennsylvania College. His nickname was Homer. The school received its charter and initial financing from the Commonwealth of Pennsylvania. Thaddeus Stevens was an early supporter of the school. Hopkins, the African-American custodian at Pennsylvania College working on the Underground Railroad, would keep Stevens informed of what was taking place at the college. J. Howard was a member of a secret fraternity not sanctioned by the college known as Beta Delta—or Black Ducks. In fact, he was one of the leaders of the organization, a Grand Sanhedrim.

The Black Ducks were a thorn in the side of the school's administration, J. Howard wrote, and also a nuisance to agents responsible for keeping the peace in the town of Gettysburg. One of the constables was John Burns, a veteran of the War of 1812 who gained fame at Gettysburg, as at the age of sixty-nine he grabbed his rifle and joined the Union army in the fighting. The headquarters of the Black Ducks was in a spacious second story room of a modest frame building on East Middle Street, directly across from the old Methodist church, according to J. Howard. The room was called the "slums" by members of the Black Ducks. According to J. Howard, one church member said, "I am afraid there is no good done up there. They are a wild and godless crew."

One person welcomed at the Black Ducks headquarters was a man J. Howard called Manuel, who was a "dancing master." On a chilly December evening in 1859, J. Howard recalled Manuel burst into the room and said, "I've got a poor fugitive down here. Master is after him, nearly starved, we must hide him." The Black Ducks members welcomed the slave, named Jim, and gave him food and drink.

Manuel said he found Jim "rushing aimlessly" in Gettysburg's streets, as his master and a government officer were searching shanties on the lane back of Washington Street. Jim had been in one of the shanties before fleeing. The Black Ducks had planned to keep Jim in their room, but as J. Howard entered the headquarters someone suggested taking him to a cave that only five members of the Black Ducks knew. Manuel was told to leave, but insisted he wanted to make sure Jim was secure.

The location was on Culp's Hill. Two rocks were parallel with each other, about five feet apart, and rose ten feet high. The Black Ducks worked hard on the secret hiding place, as they walled-up one end and the other was against the ground to a level with the top of the rocks. A roof was constructed with heavy corn wood. All of the work was covered with earth and leaves. There was only one carefully concealed entrance.

The Black Ducks gathered food and blankets and took the fugitive to the cave. The slave catchers spent two frustrating days searching in Gettysburg for Jim, who had seemingly escaped into thin air. Jim spent the two days at the cave on the summit of the windswept hill before being forwarded to Quakers in York Springs. He was then sent to Harrisburg.

Word of Manuel and the Black Ducks saving Jim soon spread among the African-American population and more came to them for help. J. Howard wrote, "It was indeed a rarity for a week to pass without some Negro appearing, in great haste, with the query, 'Whar's Massa Manuel? Must see him right away.'"

The location of the cave was kept secret by Manuel and the Black Ducks.

During the Battle of Gettysburg three members of the Black Ducks, including J. Howard, were on Culp's Hill. One Black Duck, Rubin Howerter of the 147th Pennsylvania, died in the vicinity of the slave refuge. J. Howard recalled breastworks were constructed at the cave and the roof was ruined during the fierce fighting at Culp's Hill.

J. Howard had an opportunity to experience the South's views on slavery and relations with the North immediately prior to the Civil War, as he visited a number of southern cities, including Charleston, South Carolina; Montgomery, Alabama; Memphis, Tennessee; Jackson, Mississippi; Baton Rouge, Louisiana; and Columbia, South Carolina. The Wert family owned land in the South as payment for service in the American Revolution and J. Howard traveled to the cities while collecting rent money.

J. Howard wrote letters to friends in New York City detailing what he observed during those trips. Those letters were printed in New York newspapers, but his name was never attached to the letters. If his identity was known he would have been in jeopardy of losing his life during his subsequent southern trips. Indeed, while in southern cities he heard some of his letters read out loud from New York newspapers with the readers vowing death to the writer.

During the Civil War newspapers would continue to publish reports J. Howard wrote while serving with the militia and the Army of the Potomac.

The Wert family continued helping freed slaves, even during the Civil War. J. Howard wrote about roads around his family home being full of fleeing slaves and former slaves fleeing toward the Susquehanna River as the Confederates invaded Pennsylvania. On the evening of June 20, 1863, less than two weeks before the Battle of Gettysburg, J. Howard recalled his father hearing a family of thirteen crying out for help. The family had become lost and caught in a triangle of land that had deep water surrounding it. Only one narrow path led to safety. Adam Wert rescued the family and sent them on their way to the Susquehanna and safety.

J. Howard wrote that the fleeing family had prepared for the trip by bringing along a "featherbed, two quilts, two blankets, one ham, and one ham bone that had seen better days, one rope of onions, four loaves of home-baked bread of colossal size, one frying skillet, a set of tablespoons, ditto teaspoons, a lot of knives and forks, a much worn butcher knife, a family Bible, a marriage certificate, and a framed picture of Abraham Lincoln." Adam Wert traded a more usable knife for the worn butcher knife.

J. Howard believed the family was probably from Maryland and were the last known passengers on Gettysburg's Underground Railroad.

The non-profit organization The Journey Through Hallowed Ground Partnership has published additional information, including reports by J. Howard, on the early history of Gettysburg abolitionists, the Black Ducks, and John "Jack" Hopkins.

According to the partnership, Lutheran minister Daniel Alexander Payne operated a school for black children at Pennsylvania College and found that the faculty of the college and Gettysburg Seminary supported the end of slavery and stood "ready to counsel, assist and instruct both night and day."

Hopkins was born in Maryland in 1806, appointed custodian of Pennsylvania College in 1847, and continued in the position until his death in 1868. He was well-liked by students and was called the "vice president" of the college. He married Julie Ann and they had three children: John, Wilson, and Mary. They owned a home at 219 South Washington Street, but also previously lived at a house on the college grounds. During the Civil War John Hopkins served in Company F of the 25th US Colored Troops, attaining the rank of sergeant.

The partnership reported the Beta Deltas were a group of thirty-three Pennsylvania College students—members of classes 1858–1862—who formed an unofficial and unsanctioned fraternity at the college. The cave used by the Black Ducks was called the Dowse-the-Glim Cave and was originally intended for use only by Black Duck members.

Wert Collection Anti-slavery Artifacts

Andiron in the form of a Negro woman used by Adam and Catherine Wert at their farm Wolf's Walk.

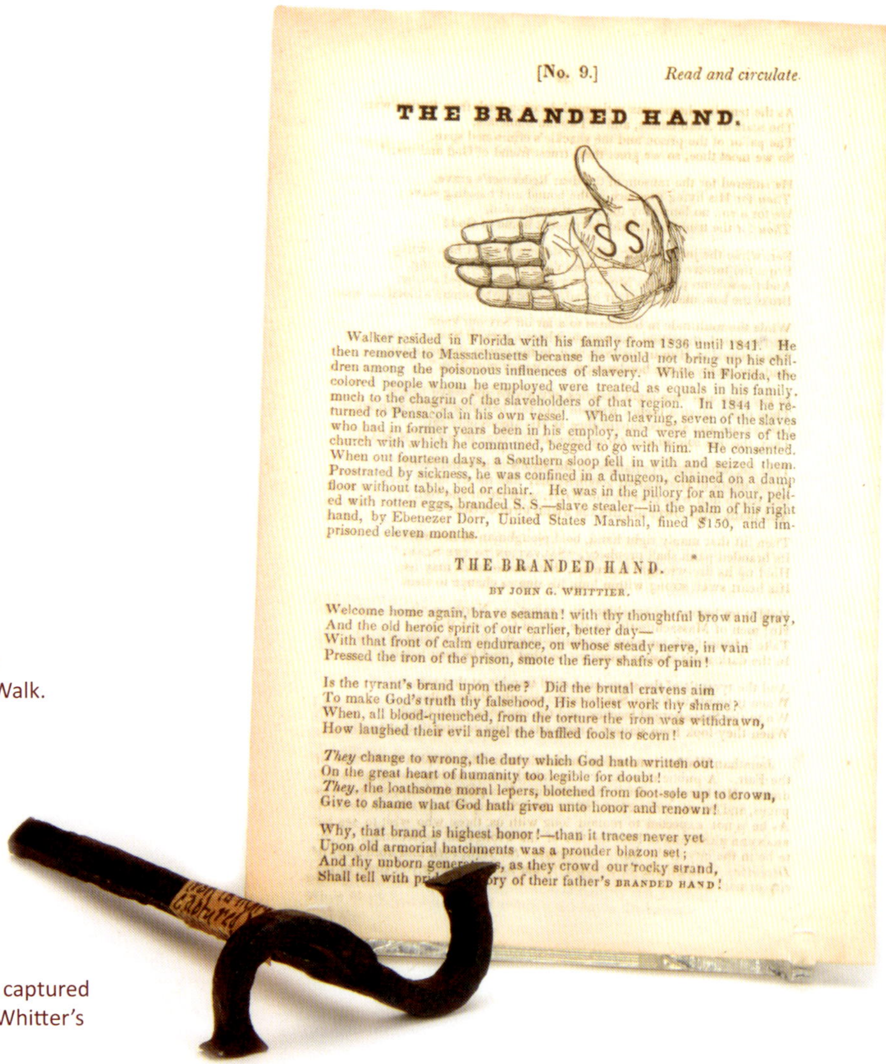

[No. 9.] *Read and circulate.*

THE BRANDED HAND.

Walker resided in Florida with his family from 1836 until 1841. He then removed to Massachusetts because he would not bring up his children among the poisonous influences of slavery. While in Florida, the colored people whom he employed were treated as equals in his family, much to the chagrin of the slaveholders of that region. In 1844 he returned to Pensacola in his own vessel. When leaving, seven of the slaves who had in former years been in his employ, and were members of the church with which he communed, begged to go with him. He consented. When out fourteen days, a Southern sloop fell in with and seized them. Prostrated by sickness, he was confined in a dungeon, chained on a damp floor without table, bed or chair. He was in the pillory for an hour, pelted with rotten eggs, branded S. S.—slave stealer—in the palm of his right hand, by Ebenezer Dorr, United States Marshal, fined $150, and imprisoned eleven months.

THE BRANDED HAND.

BY JOHN G. WHITTIER.

Welcome home again, brave seaman! with thy thoughtful brow and gray,
And the old heroic spirit of our earlier, better day—
With that front of calm endurance, on whose steady nerve, in vain
Pressed the iron of the prison, smote the fiery shafts of pain!

Is the tyrant's brand upon thee? Did the brutal cravens aim
To make God's truth thy falsehood, His holiest work thy shame?
When, all blood-quenched, from the torture the iron was withdrawn,
How laughed their evil angel the baffled fools to scorn!

They change to wrong, the duty which God hath written out
On the great heart of humanity too legible for doubt!
They, the loathsome moral lepers, blotched from foot-sole up to crown,
Give to shame what God hath given unto honor and renown!

Why, that brand is highest honor!—than it traces never yet
Upon old armorial hatchments was a prouder blazon set;
And thy unborn gene[illegible], as they crowd our rocky strand,
Shall tell with pr[illegible]ry of their father's BRANDED HAND!

Slave "S" branding iron used to mark captured runaway slaves, and John Greenleaf Whitter's famous poem "Branded Hand."

Painting on wood board of John Greenleaf Whitter's *Kneeling Slave in Chains*.

Patriotic framed portrait of Lydia Hamilton Smith, Thaddeus Stevens's administrative assistant. A descendant of the Hamiltons that settled along the Adams County mountains in 1739, Lydia was known as "Gettysburg's Colored Heroine," as she gathered supplies for the wounded soldiers and prayed with them in the field hospitals. She was fifty years old in 1863. An anti-slavery blue wafer printed with a religious verse is in the case to the left.

Walking stick from the last trip on the Underground Railroad on June 20, 1863, before the Battle of Gettysburg. The stick was given to Adam Wert for his assistance helping slaves escape.

A rare outdoor ambrotype of a Negro boy delivering a wagon of fence rails.

Anti-slavery code book used by the Black Ducks of Pennsylvania College, and a photograph of Wolf Hill, where slaves were hidden.

First edition custom leather bound *Uncle Tom's Cabin* shows Harriet Beecher Stowe's vision of Christ liberating the slaves which motivated her to write the book. The brass paper clip held Mrs. Stowe's notes during the writing of this American classic.

A Staffordshire figurine made in England of characters from *Uncle Tom's Cabin*. The porcelain figurine was made in the 1850s to raise money to fight slavery.

This anti-slavery grouping includes Old Uncle Ned Songster, Black Duck passes, a telescope, and J. Howard Wert's winter lamb's wool gloves.

Chapter Four

J. HOWARD WERT'S BATTLE OF GETTYSBURG

J. Howard participated in the epic battle of Gettysburg. He knew and conversed with the major participants of the three-day engagement that saved the Union. Throughout the following years he often spoke to groups about the battle and wrote a number of articles and books on Gettysburg.

For the fiftieth anniversary of the conflict he wrote a fifty-three-page booklet, *Historical Souvenir of the Fiftieth Anniversary of the Battle of Gettysburg*. The booklet was published by the *Harrisburg Telegraph* and credit for the manuscript was given to "Prof. J. Howard Wert, Historian and Late Lieutenant Penna. Volunteers."

The booklet gives J. Howard's observations on the battle, recounts many individual struggles, and lists details of the armies that took part in the three days of fighting in July 1863 at Gettysburg. J. Howard wrote that Gettysburg ranks as one of the earth's decisive battles and was the greatest battle of a great Civil War. The victory won by Union forces under Gen. George G. Meade was the turning point of the war for the suppression of the rebellion. J. Howard gave credit to the rebel soldiers, saying at Gettysburg "Southern valor reached its highest swell of daring and from that time the cause of the Southland ebbed until it reached the surrender of Appomattox."

The three days of fighting and death left a lasting impression on J. Howard:

> The fierce onsets of opposing hosts, the rows of heaped and mangled dead along right and left and center, all the splendors and all the horror of those three crucial days in July 1863 have been impressed on the memory of the writer with a vividness naught can efface. With equal distinctness come the succeeding months of the hospital period as he [J. Howard] daily wandered over different portions of the field and conversed with hundreds of wounded and often dying men from Maine to far away Minnesota on the west and Texas on the south. He comes then to you, readers, as an eyewitness to tell the story of Gettysburg.

Emma Aughinbaugh, J. Howard Wert's future wife, waved a silk flag during the engagement, greeting Buford's Cavalry the evening before the battle, and used the towel caring for the wounded.

A patriotic song scrapbook used by Emma Aughinbaugh when Union soldiers rode into Gettysburg.

As for the Southern forces of Gen. Robert E. Lee, J. Howard writes, "On this globe no body of better disciplined or braver men have ever responded to the roll of the drum than the 85,000 in Gray that Lee dashed against the granite cliffs of Gettysburg held by the Army of the Potomac. He had confidence in them, and they unbounded confidence in him."

J. Howard begins his narrative on June 26, when advancing Confederate troops first entered Gettysburg and skirmished with a small body of troops from Pennsylvania south of the town. He recounted the first Union soldier to die was George Washington Sandoe, a member of a local cavalry company. Sandoe died on the property of James McAllister, one of the anti-slavery leaders of Gettysburg. McAllister watched the fighting from his mill and ran to see the condition of young Sandoe. J. Howard wrote that McAllister then reprimanded the Confederates for shooting Sandoe and the Confederates replied they only wanted his horse.

The two units disengaged, and four days later a portion of the main Union army reached Gettysburg. Gen. John Buford's division of cavalry occupied the low ridges just west of town between Seminary Ridge and Marsh Creek. On June 30, Buford's men rode through the streets of Gettysburg. Citizens of the town, boys and girls, lined Washington Street, waved flags, and sang patriotic songs. The three-day battle of Gettysburg was about to commence.

The next day Buford's troops engaged units of Confederate Gen. A. P. Hill as they advanced down the Chambersburg Pike. J. Howard was busy leading Union units to positions on the

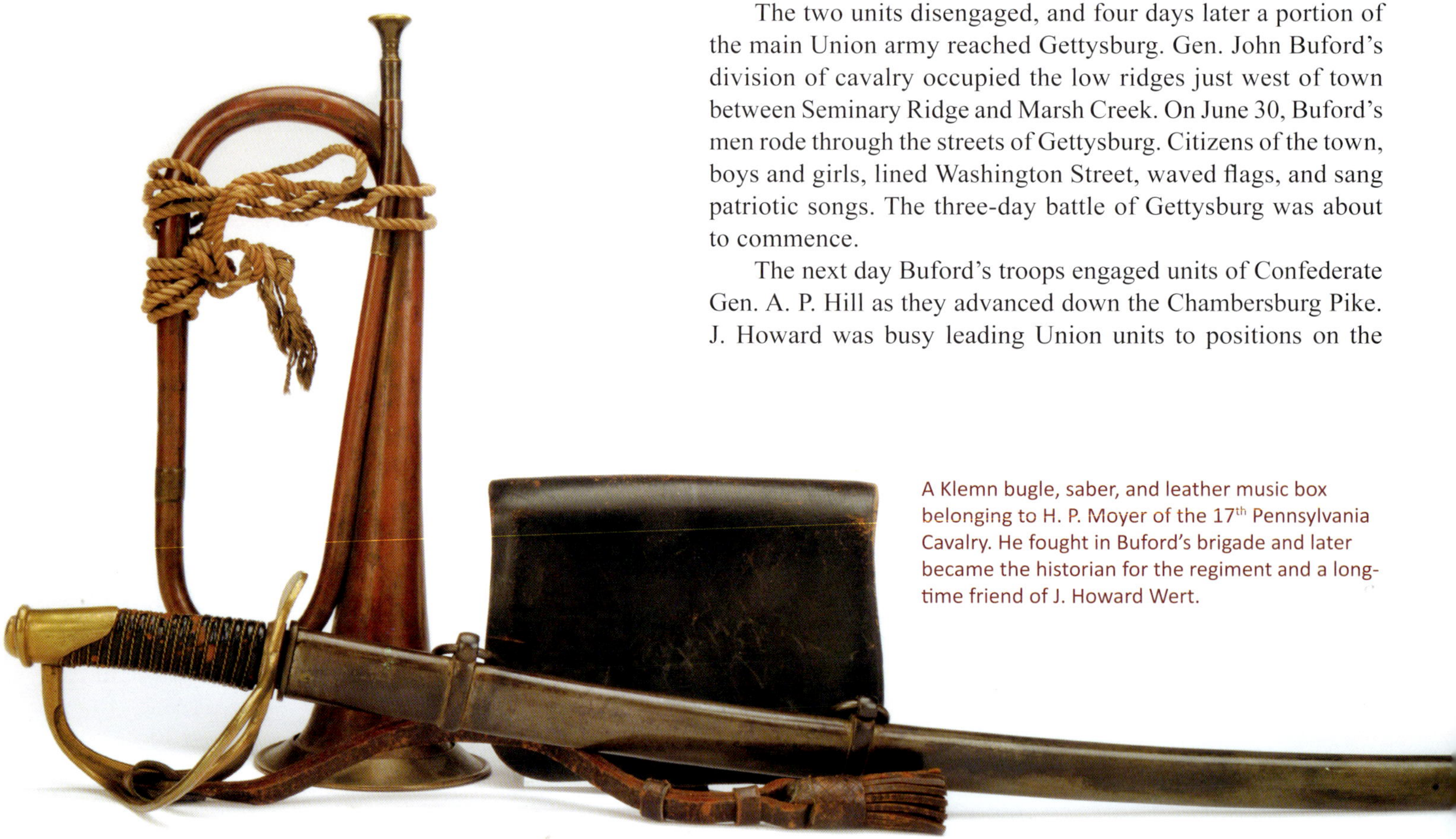

A Klemn bugle, saber, and leather music box belonging to H. P. Moyer of the 17th Pennsylvania Cavalry. He fought in Buford's brigade and later became the historian for the regiment and a long-time friend of J. Howard Wert.

battlefield when he saw the Union's First Corps, under the command of Gen. John F. Reynolds of Pennsylvania, enter the fight. J. Howard wrote:

> I never saw a grander sight on any field of battle than the First Corps rushing into action that balmy summer morning. Behind them, double-quicking from the Emmittsburg Road, and rapidly forming their line of battle along Seminary Ridge, came as far as eye could reach, a line of loyal blue and glittering steel. All around was a charming landscape of peace and plenty. Waving harvest fields and meadows of richest green were blended in the fairy view.

The fairy view J. Howard described would soon become a scene of desolation, as he wrote:

> happy homesteads would be charred ruins, that all the verdant fields would be a trodden mass of mire, darkly dyed with crimson, and that for weary miles the earth would show no fruitage upon its bosom but mutilated corpses.

J. Howard went on to describe the six hours of fighting by the First Corps against Hill's Confederates. Every ridge, grove, and railroad cut was fought over again and again according to J. Howard. The desperate fighting at close quarters took place in open field, with no protection for the soldiers of either side. Reynolds was the first Union general to die at Gettysburg.

The fighting took place on ground J. Howard explored as a child, and also on the land of family friends, including Thaddeus Stevens. J. Howard said part of the day's conflict took place at Stevens's unfinished Tapeworm railroad.

Hill's Confederates advanced from Cashtown, to the west of Gettysburg, to meet the Union soldiers. J. Howard reported: "The first screaming shell that flew across Seminary Ridge July 1 effectively closed the collegiate work of the day [at Pennsylvania

Shoulder valise, dust brush, telescope, and signal flags belonging to Lt. Aaron D. Jerome, chief signal officer of Gen. John Buford's First Cavalry Division. Buford established an observation station in the cupola of the Lutheran Theological Seminary.

Gen. Reynolds' dried flower coffin wreath used at his funeral in Lancaster, Pennsylvania.

A broken foot officer's sword and cased ambrotype of a woman belonging to Lt. Col. Samuel G. Shepard of the 7th Tennessee of Archer's Brigade. The sword was found near where Archer's men surrendered on July 1, 1863, and was decorated with a red-white-blue custom-made sword knot.

College] and before night the few [students] that remained saw shattered regiments in blue solemnly retreating before the foe in gray."

Those first shells were a sign to Reynolds that he had to advance to the assistance of Buford. Reynolds then sent messages to Gens. Oliver O. Howard and Dan Sickles to advance on Gettysburg. J. Howard wrote: "If there is a brigade that above and beyond all others is entwined in the writer's memory with feeling of profoundest vernation, it is the Iron Brigade, the first brigade of the first division of the first corps. They were placed in a grove by Reynolds himself just before the general fell."

J. Howard wrote about two of the first Union units that engaged the Confederates: the 14th New York, known as the 14th Brooklyn, of Maj. Gen. Lysander Cutler's brigade, at the railroad cut; and the Black Hats of the Iron Brigade from the Midwest. On the south part of the Chambersburg Road near Willoughby Run was where Confederate Gen. James Archer was captured and later transported to the Union prison at Fort Delaware, a dozen miles south of Wilmington, Delaware.

J. Howard noted members of Cutler's brigade, the 56th Pennsylvania under the command of Col. J. W. Hoffman, fired the first infantry volley that opened the battle. The brigade included the 7th Indiana, the 14th, 76th, 95th, and 147th New York, and the 56th Pennsylvania. Cutler's brigade fought the numerically superior Confederates for hours on the fields west of Gettysburg.

Joining the Black Hats of the Iron Brigade and the 14th Brooklyn on the field was Capt. James Hall and his Second Maine artillery. Gen. Abner Doubleday ordered Hall to hold the area

Capt. James A. Hall's kepi, cameo portrait, and sword with a lady liberty watch fob dangling from the hilt. Hall commanded the 2nd Maine Battery.

Items recovered near the 2nd Maine position of July 1, include an artillery valise, photo, spurs, part of a Confederate shell, an artillery vent pick, patriotic cover, knife, a religious book, and a rebel cannon projectile fragment.

A pistol, New York belt buckle, buttons, blue pouch, and razor from the 14th New York, known as the Brooklyn Zouaves, with a note saying J. Howard Wert picked up the items on the battlefield on July 13, 1863.

near McPherson's Ridge at all costs. Confederates charged Hall's guns, shouting their famed rebel yell. "With double-shotted charges Hall blew them from the muzzles of his guns. The slopes in his front were covered with their dead," J. Howard wrote:

> On some portions of the field so many of the Confederates had fallen that their bodies formed a partial rampart for the protection of others. Coming up, prone behind these corpses, they picked off the Union gunners.
>
> Once, twice repulsed, on the Confederates came, again and again. Ever relentless against the service of grape and canister. Finally the enemy was on and over Hall's guns. His men fought them hand to hand. The foe clubbed their muskets. The Maine men beat them off with stones, cannon rammers and any missiles that came by their hand. Hall's artillery brought off four of their six cannons, dragging them by hand to their new line a mile distant.

About 5:00 p.m., Hall's command went along the Baltimore Pike near the Wert home to be refitted. Members of the unit went to the Wert farm to secure horses and hay. As the sun descended J. Howard told members of the Second Maine that milk could be obtained from the family cows, and soon a crowd gathered to attempt to obtain the scarce commodity.

J. Howard made note of huge losses of one Confederate regiment, the 26th Carolina. The regiment entered July 1 with 800 men and was one of the largest Confederate regiments. By the end of the first day they had lost 708 casualties. This was the greatest loss of any one regiment on either side during the Civil War. The unit lost eighty-six killed, 502 wounded, and 120 missing.

Also on McPherson's Ridge were members of the Pennsylvania Bucktails, the 143rd, 149th, and 150th Pennsylvania. For five hours the Pennsylvanians fought the Confederates. At the railroad cut north of the Chambersburg Pike the 149th Pennsylvania gave the Confederates a withering fire. The Rebels kept charging and the Bucktails fired in their foe's faces and charged them with their bayonets. The Southerners retreated, but the Bucktails were forced to return to their original battle line under heavy Confederate artillery fire. Two Union commanders—Cols. Roy Stone and Langhorne Wister—were wounded during the fighting. Wister was shot through both cheeks and for the rest of his life wore a beard to cover the scar.

The Bucktails fell back to Seminary Ridge, where in late afternoon a determined attempt to stop the Confederates' advance was made. In due time the Confederates overwhelmed the Union

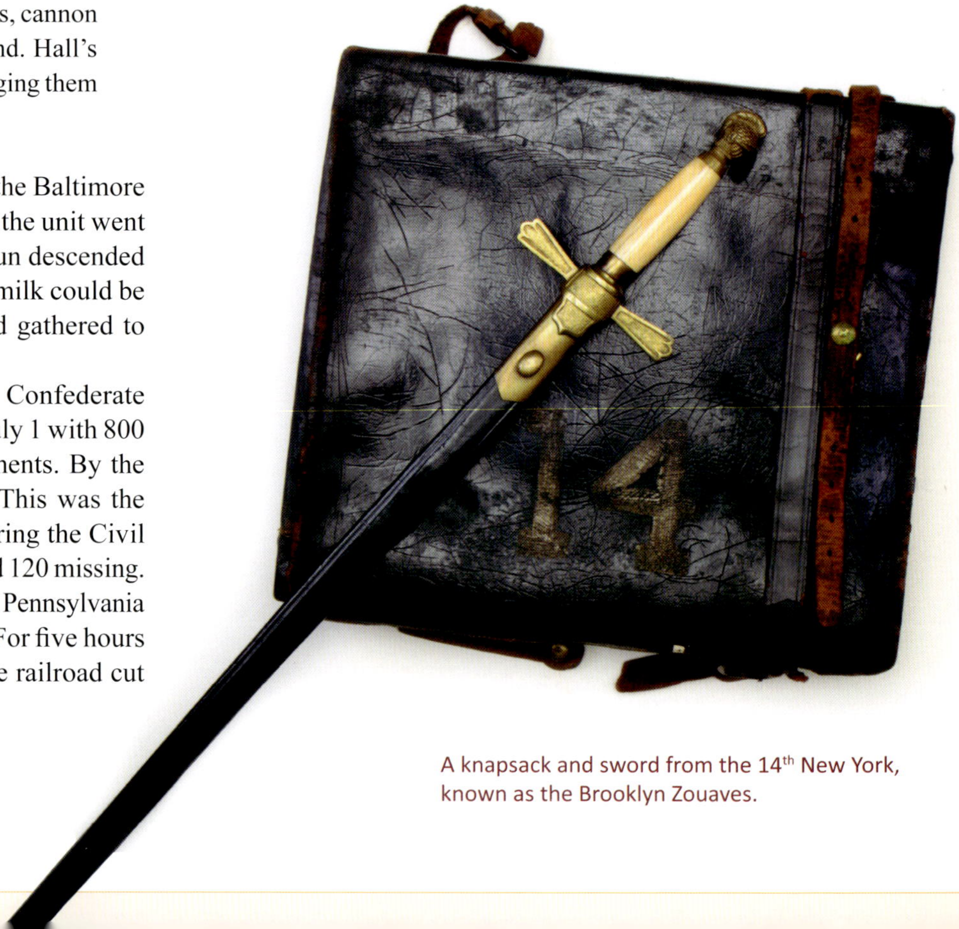

A knapsack and sword from the 14th New York, known as the Brooklyn Zouaves.

A kepi from the 14th New York.

Artifacts from the 26th North Carolina include items from a first sergeant writing reports for the unit, a pepper box pistol, ink well, and a line designator for writing on un-ruled paper. The report indicated the first sergeant was wounded during the first day's fighting.

A small field desk, music stand, keyed flute, and NCO sword from the 26th North Carolina.

Coverlet, leather strap, and buckle of James B. Jordan, 26th North Carolina.

defenders and the remaining Bucktails became part of the general Union retreat to Cemetery Ridge.

One section of J. Howard's sketch dealt with heroes of the first day, including Union Gen. Gabriel Rene Paul, who was seriously wounded in the left eye fighting at Oak Ridge and left for dead. His injuries left him totally blind and with severely impaired senses of hearing and smell. J. Howard reported that for many years after the war his loving daughter guided him through the streets of Washington.

Another hero recognized by J. Howard was John Burns. J. Howard wrote:

> All though these bloody hours an aged citizen of Gettysburg, of humble station in life, was winning an immortality of fame. A soldier in the war of 1812, he had made repeated, but unavailing efforts to enlist in the Union army. Now, when the storm of battle came thundering to his own door, he took down ancient fowling piece and joining one of the battling regiments of the First Corps, the Bucktails, began firing at the enemy.

Pennsylvania Bucktail document box belonging to Gen. Langhorne Wisters, commander of the Bucktail Brigade, who was wounded at McPherson's Ridge.

Burns was wounded multiple times and Confederates returned Burns to his own home.

The fighting the first day intensified, as two divisions of Confederate Gen. Richard S. Ewell and Howard's Union 11th Corps joined the conflict. Howard's men marched through the streets of Gettysburg by way of Carlisle Street and were greeted by maids and matrons giving water, according to J. Howard. Those same Union soldiers would soon retreat past those maids and maidens, as the combined forces of the First and 11th Corps were not enough to thwart the massed Southern forces. Many of Howard's men were shot and captured in the town. Survivors of the First Corps were able to withdraw through the open fields west of Gettysburg and did so in good order. J. Howard wrote:

> Thoughtful and anxious in that hour of doubt and dread, [Gen.] Meade hurried [Gen. Winfield] Hancock forward to take command on July 1 and with a glance Hancock took in the whole situation. The advantages and its dangers in five minutes time had been resolved that there on the natural rampart, extending from Culp's hill to the round tops that the battle Reynolds had started should be finished.

The magic presence of Hancock restored confidence in the exhausted troops of the 1st and 11th Corps J. Howard wrote, with Hancock realigning the troops in a strong defensive position.

J. Howard singled out individual stories throughout his article and wrote about Lt. Bayard Wilkeson, an eighteen-year-old member of the US Army commanding a battery. He fought at Barlow's Knob, where thirty-six Confederate cannons took aim. "Through all the screaming rain of shell he sat on his horse unmoved to encourage his men," J. Howard wrote. A shell smashed Wilkeson's leg, and after using his sash as a tourniquet he took his own knife to his leg to amputate it. One of his men found water for the officer, but he gave the water to a wounded man

A Pennsylvania Bucktail kepi.

Binoculars and case belonging to Gen. Oliver O. Howard. A note from Howard to J. Howard Wert says, "With kind regards, Maj. General O. O. Howard."

Lt. Bayard Wilkeson's photograph and telescope are shown with his wallet.

who drank all the liquid. Wilkeson was carried to the nearby Adams County almshouse, where he was captured by the Confederates. J. Howard describes his death, "That night, in a little room of the dreary building, alone and uncared for, the soul of that young hero, Bayard Wilkeson, took its flight, whilst a mile away, as the crow flies, his aged father was wringing his hands in helpless grief."

Wilkeson's father was *New York Times* reporter Samuel Wilkeson. The reporter arrived on the field the night of July 1. In his dispatch on the battle Wilkeson wrote of his son, "crushed by a shell in a position where a battery should never have been sent, and abandoned to death in a building where surgeons dared not to stay." In the same article reporter Wilkeson wrote of a second birth of freedom in America.

Confederate losses were also described by J. Howard. He wrote of Confederate Gen. Alfred Iverson believing his dead troops were alive and surrendering. "When I saw white handkerchiefs raised and my line of battle still lying down in position, I characterized the surrender as disgraceful; but when I found afterwards that 500 of my men were left lying dead and wounded in a line as straight as a dress parade, I exonerated the survivors and claim for the brigade that they nobly fought and died."

On the same day Union Gen. Francis Barlow was saved by Confederate Gen. John B. Gordon. J. Howard gave a brief description of the incident, but Gordon wrote a more detailed account in his book *Reminiscences of the Civil War*. Gordon remembers discovering Barlow on his back, surrounded by Union

A Confederate vest from an officer's haversack and a pistol from the Iverson Pits area of Oak Ridge.

A haversack covered in red fox fur with a carrying strap belonging to a Rebel officer in Iverson's unit, plus a silver snuff box engraved with a shield.

A Confederate leather canteen with oil cloth strap and a prayer book found at Iverson Pits.

Silver rosettes and an engraved bit from Gen. Francis Barlow's horse.

Gen. Francis Barlow's silver mounted saddle, pistol holsters, and campaign saddle blanket.

dead. Gordon believed Barlow was near death, as he was shot through the chest and the ball exited near his spinal cord, paralyzing his legs and arms. Barlow asked Gordon if he ever met Mrs. Barlow that he tell her his last thoughts were of her. Under a flag of truce Gordon sent a message to Mrs. Barlow that night and offered to escort her to her husband. She did so and nursed Barlow back to health. Later in the war a relative of Gordon was killed and Barlow believed the man who saved him at Gettysburg had died. Fifteen years later they met in Washington by chance at a dinner. "I asked Barlow, 'General, are you related to the Barlow who was killed at Gettysburg?' He replied: 'Why, I am the man, sir. Are you related to the Gordon who killed me?' 'I am the man, sir,' I responded." The two men became friends.

Another Union solider thought mortally wounded was Lt. Col. John B. Callis of the 7th Wisconsin. He stayed in Gettysburg for weeks after the battle, nursed by his wife. When Callis insisted on being taken home a surgeon said, "Take him. He will die on the way, but he will die if he remains." Callis was taken by railroad to his home and lived for many years, although always suffering from his wounds.

J. Howard wrote about another incident that became famous throughout the country. This event took place within a stone's throw from where J. Howard lived for years on York Street. A dead Union soldier was found, and in his grasp was a photograph of "three sweet, innocent little children." His identity was unknown at the time. After the battle philanthropist George W. Childs of the *Philadelphia Ledger* had thousands of copies of the photo made and distributed to help identify him. Eventually the Cattaraugus County, New York, children of Sgt. Amos Humiston of the 154th New York of the 11th Corps were recognized. Copies of the photograph were sold and proceeds were used to help start the orphans' home in Gettysburg.

One of the roads in Gettysburg today is Steinwehr Avenue. The street is named after Gen. Adolph Von Steinwehr of the 11th Corps. Baron Adolph Wilhelm August Friedrich von Steinwehr was a skilled engineer who served in the Prussian army. During the afternoon of the first day's fighting his men strengthened stone fences around Cemetery Hill which would serve as protection for the Union infantry during the next two days of fighting.

Summing up the first day at Gettysburg, J. Howard gave credit to the Federal cavalry, especially Buford. "Without Buford's resolute and skillful delays of the enemy's advance on the first day, and the cavalry battles on the extreme right and left wings of the Army of the Potomac at a subsequent period in the battle, the result at Gettysburg might have been vastly different."

During the evening of July 1, J. Howard visited some of the wounded men, especially at the hospital set up for the First Corps on the Baltimore Pike at Mark's Church. The church was across the street from where J. Howard lived. He wrote about the heroes of the Iron Brigade and noted that those noble men were on cots of suffering and that was where he learned to love them. The nation owed a debt of gratitude to those soldiers of the First Corps, according to J. Howard.

The Gettysburg residents who failed to flee before the fighting had to spend much of the following two days in their cellars as the fighting raged above and around them. The civilians were not alone, as survivors of the 11th Corps also sought refuge when they found an open door or window in private homes. Even though the Confederates searched for Union soldiers, many of the boys were successfully hidden by town residents, noted J. Howard. One such soldier was wounded Union Gen. Alex Schimmelfenning.

Food was scarce for the inhabitants, as the Confederate soldiers confiscated all that they could find. The residents most in danger, recalled J. Howard, were the ones living on the southern part of Baltimore Street near the cemetery. Houses there were occupied by sharpshooters of both armies. They kept up a constant exchange day and night, and every shutter and external door in this vicinity was pierced with from ten to twenty bullet holes in J. Howard's estimate. When residents ventured from the cellars they at times found dead men in their parlors and bedrooms.

J. Howard called the night of July 1 a sad one for the town of Gettysburg. He said dead men were strewn throughout the town, and many streets had barricades hastily constructed of paving stones, demolished fences, and furniture taken from homes. The Theological Seminary on the ridge west of Gettysburg was turned into a hospital, as was Pennsylvania College. In fact, J. Howard wrote that every school house, church, and private home was used to treat the wounded. "The livelong night the air was heavy with the moans of pain and the shrieks of anguish."

Citizens did what they could to help the suffering men. Some braved the ongoing battle to take supplies to the wounded. One Union chaplain doing the same duty was shot dead on the steps of Christ's church on Chambersburg Street, according to J. Howard. He said some civilians suffered gunshot wounds.

Two photographs of Colonel George McFarland, along with an unused shoe from 1864 and an iron leg brace. His left leg was amputated during the first day of fighting at Gettysburg. A noted educator, he was appointed superintendent of Pennsylvania's Orphans' Schools.

Dress sword and sharkskin scabbard of Col. George McFarland of the 151st Pennsylvania.

The night was also time for the Union army to receive reinforcements. Even before darkness the head of the 12th Corps was closing on Gettysburg. As the 12th Corps was traveling on Baltimore Pike, J. Howard saw a family standing in the road with buckets of milk—all of the milk they had on their farm—to give to the passing soldiers. J. Howard was with the 12th Corps at the time, and reported that this was not an isolated case. The kindness was appreciated by the Union troops and J. Howard heard them exclaim, "Ah! We are in Pennsylvania now. Boys, this ain't Old Virginia. Oh! We can fight for a state like this." In one of his *Little Stories of Gettysburg* J. Howard wrote about Union soldiers crowding around cows on one farm waiting for drops of milk.

When the sun arose the morning of July 2, the whole Army of the Potomac had gathered and commanded a strong defensive

A mahogany box of relics of Col. Alexander Biddle, 121st Pennsylvania, containing a piece of brick from the Lutheran Theological Seminary, an officer's eagle powder flask, a Klemm and Company brass bugle, a pocket wallet, shell fragment, and a gold sword knot.

Gen. Henry Slocum's custom-made briefcase and his monogrammed fruit knife were carried in his saddlebags.

position, maybe the strongest defensive position of the entire war. Meade had a five-mile defensive line shaped like a fishhook, with its center near the knolls of Cemetery and East Cemetery Hills south of Gettysburg. The longer line of the Union defense ended at Little Round Top and Big Round Top. The shorter extension concluded at Culp's Hill. The Union soldiers spent hours building and reinforcing defensive positions along the line.

Remaining units of the Confederate army also rushed to Lee's side, and by morning all had arrived except for Gen. George Pickett's division of Longstreet's Corps. The center of Lee's line was on Seminary Ridge, the scene of fierce fighting the first day. The two armies were about a mile apart at most points.

The morning of July 2 passed fairly quietly, according to J. Howard. All changed when Union Gen. Dan Sickles led his Third Corps too far forward and was attacked by Gen. James Longstreet's rebels. "It is impossible," J. Howard wrote, "in a condensed epitome of the battle, to follow the thousand details of that constantly changing battle—afternoon of the second great engagement of Gettysburg. It was the most complicated of all the fights on this field." J. Howard noted that fighting at Devil's Den, Little Round Top, the Rose Farm and Wheatfield, and the Peach Orchard continued throughout the sultry afternoon and did not conclude until 8:00 p.m.

Hill's Confederate Corps soon joined Longstreet, and the Union Second Corps under Hancock aided Sickles. The heated contest surged across Gettysburg fields, and in the midst was a little house along the Emmitsburg Road occupied by Josephine Rogers and her mother. The two women baked bread for the soldiers, and after the war, during a reunion, one of the soldiers told the women that the sweetest food he had ever eaten was the bread baked by those two noble women under the fire of the enemy.

Another cottage on the crest of the Peach Orchard Ridge was occupied by John Wentz and his wife. They were in their eighties when the battle took place, and a son they had not seen in more than twenty years fought in their front yard with a Confederate artillery unit from New Orleans.

For many members of Company K of the First Pennsylvania Reserve regiment fighting on Little Round Top, they could also see their family homes, as they were recruited from Adams County. Sgt. Samuel A. Young walked across his family farm and had a brief conversation with his father and sisters, but did not get a chance to see his mother.

J. Howard claims the Sherfy farm's Peach Orchard was a pioneering endeavor in Southern Pennsylvania. He described the desperate struggle that took place. According to J. Howard the orchard was shot out of existence. "It had produced annually thousands of bushes of luscious fruit. There was not enough left of it to ever yield thereafter a single peach; but it garnered, that sultry afternoon, a frightful fruitage of the slain."

J. Howard also vividly described the scene at the Wheatfield, where a half dozen times soldiers from each side surged across

A silver hilted dagger belonging to Isaac Davis Stamps, who was related to Confederate President Jefferson Davis. Stamps belonged to the 21st Mississippi and died at the Peach Orchard on July 2, 1863.

A stock from a US Springfield found on the Joseph Sherfy farm on the Emmitsburg Road.

the fields and were then repulsed. "Where at noon was waving grain, in golden ripeness and luxuriance," J. Howard wrote:

> the darkness fell on heel-pressed sod that oozed forth blood, on brooklets that ran in crimson streams, on a land so thickly sown with the dying and the dead, that those who traveled on the field walked on corpses, and little wonder that it was so, for more than a score of brigades in Blue and Gray had met in their wrath and there had sternly wrestled for the mastery.

The scenes at the Wheatfield deeply affected J. Howard, as he recalled his visits there in the days following the battle. He wrote:

> A battle has never yet been described by the most brilliant writer so as to give the reader a full conception of its intensity of both splendor and horror. It must be seen and experienced to be understood. But if the most skilled of word painters have failed to describe adequately the rage of battle, how utter must be the failure to depict the field of conflict when the passionate strife has ceased—when the splendor, the pomp, and the circumstance of battle's magnificent stern array have gone, and only the horrible remains in its ghastliest and most terrible forms.
>
> The writer of this history [J. Howard] was over the Wheatfield and the adjacent battle line, July 5, 1863, and many subsequent days of that month. No words can portray the awful picture of desolation, devastation, and death present.

Across the field was the debris of battle: broken muskets, soiled bayonets, shattered ammunition chests, blood-defiled clothing, trodden cartridge boxes, splintered swords, rifled knapsacks, and battered canteens. "Everywhere death, and death in its most abhorrent forms!"

A Confederate riding crop and rare horse blanket from the Rose farm.

A Confederate blanket, bayonet, and part of a musket found in the Wheatfield.

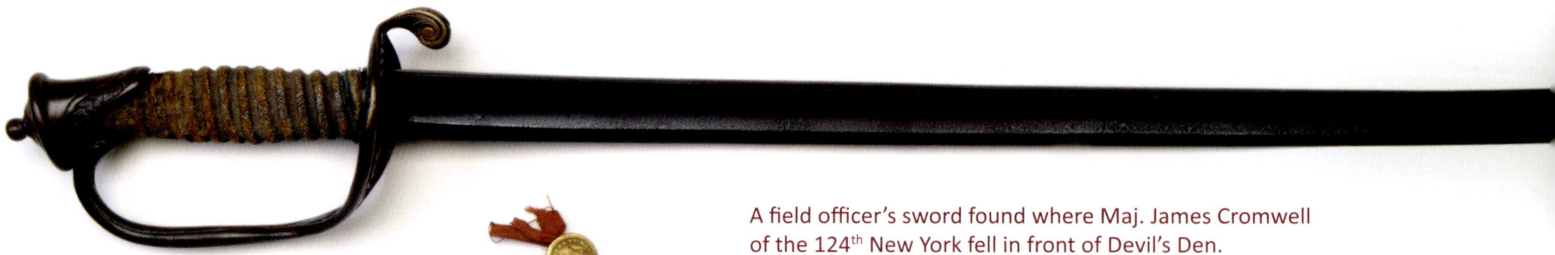

A field officer's sword found where Maj. James Cromwell of the 124th New York fell in front of Devil's Den.

J. Howard also described the discovery of more than 150 dead Confederates near Devil's Den in the days after the battle. A heavy rain unearthed shoes, hats, locks of hair, and portions of the soldiers' bodies. He wrote about the sorrow in many Southern families:

> Alas! In how many Southern homes aching hearts, waited through weary months for news of loved ones that never came, until the void of suspense was replaced by the dread certainty that the absent one had helped to swell the unknown dead of the Wheatfield in a Northern land!

A more peaceful moment was observed when Father William Corby prayed with the Second Corps' Irish Brigade. The soldiers from the Massachusetts, New York, and Pennsylvania regiments kneeled in a rocky ravine as Father Corby used the massive rocks of the gorge as his pulpit and pronounced a blessing and absolution. "Now, forward boys, and do your duty to God and your country," J. Howard quoted the priest as saying.

The fighting done by Longstreet's Corps, at the end of the day, did not advance the Southern position. Also, Lee's attempts at Culp's Hill and East Cemetery Hill failed to break the Union's lines. J. Howard described the desperate struggle to save the battery of Union officer Bruce Rickett, where Pennsylvania soldiers said they would rather die on their own soil than surrender their guns.

J. Howard singled out one Union officer—Gen. Winfield Scott Hancock—for special recognition, calling him a genius of war. The next day J. Howard wrote that Meade would call Hancock "The Superb," as Hancock was felled by a wound. "From the time the fight opened on July 2 Hancock was here, there, everywhere that disaster threatened," J. Howard wrote.

As night fell on July 2, 1863, a soldier wounded during the fighting at Little Round Top made his way to the Wert homestead south of Gettysburg. The soldier wanted to bathe his wounded arm and later bedded down under a table where officers came throughout the night for coffee, bread, and a look at a map of Adams County hanging on the wall. In the morning J. Howard's mother gave the soldier a sandwich and a cup of coffee. The soldier insisted he had a "lovely wound" because he would be able to carry a musket again in a week. He was last seen heading toward a hospital.

As the day began, George Slagle, a Gettysburg resident, gave up on his attempts to end the fighting. Slagle was a pious man who lived about four miles from town, and for the previous two days he prayed to God to stop the fighting. On that Friday morning he told his family he would pray no more about the battle, as the armies were fighting earlier in the day and louder than the previous day.

Slagle was hearing the battle raging at Culp's Hill, where Confederate Gen. Edward Johnson's division was battling the Union 12th Corps. Earlier in the morning members of both armies took water from Spangler's Spring, but now they were fighting for control of the important hill that was the right flank of the Union army. For seven hours the battle raged through the fine oak forest known for years as Gettysburg's favorite picnic grounds. The area was no longer suitable for social gatherings.

On nearby Culp's Hill neighbor battled neighbor, as Maryland units recruited from the same part of the state were engaged, some fighting for the North and some for the South, "But such is a civil war," J. Howard penned. A schoolmate of J. Howard, Wesley Culp, went south in his early manhood and returned to Culp's Hill to fight with the Confederate army. "Culp was a common and honorable name in the Gettysburg of that day," J. Howard wrote. "Young

Confederate cartridge box, 37th Virginia canteen, and a Confederate wrapper from Richmond with a note saying found on Culp's Hill.

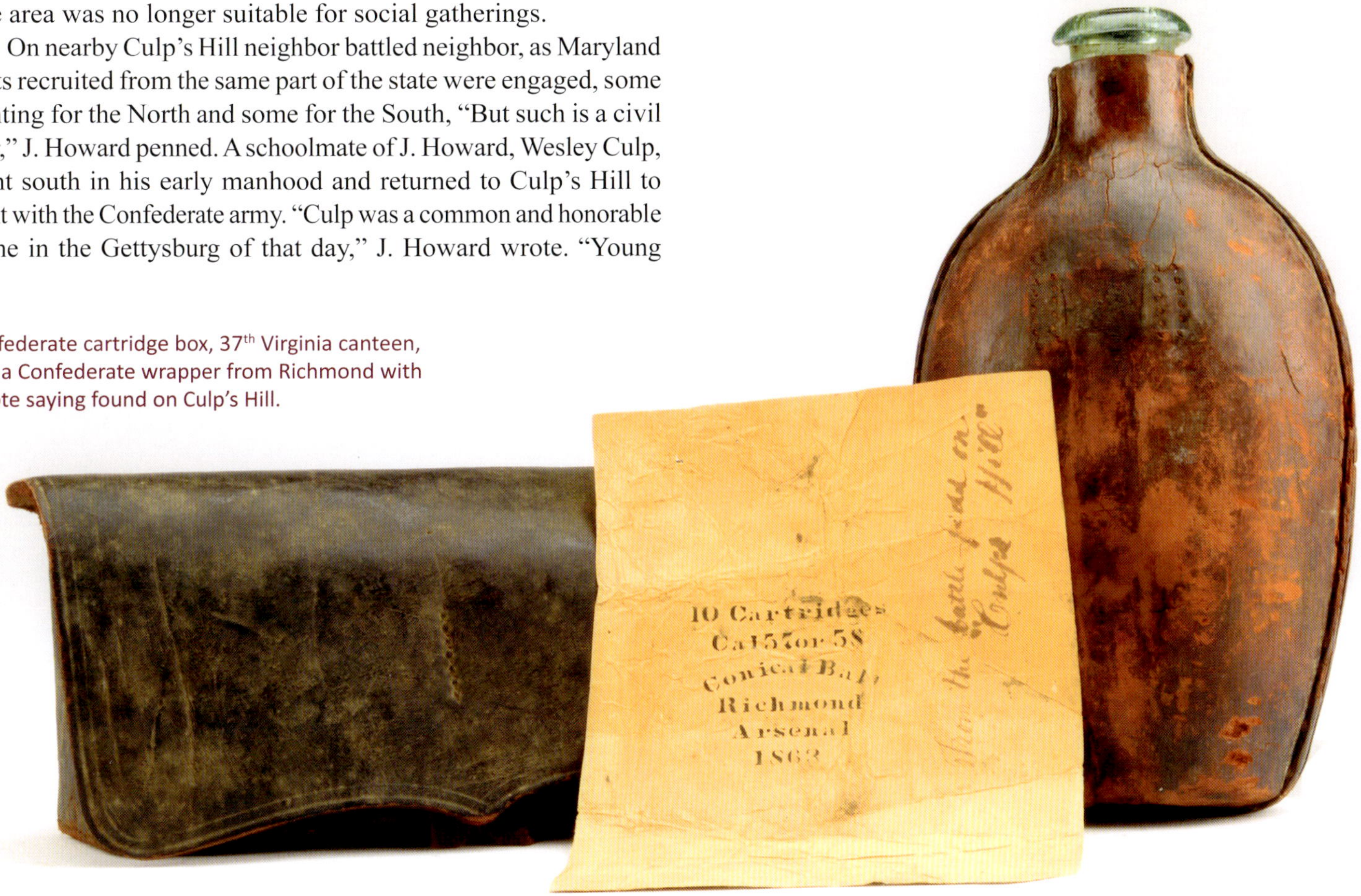

Folk art carved on wood of Gens. George Meade and Winfield Hancock meeting on July 2, 1863, by an unknown artist.

Formal sword of Union Gen. John Geary of the 12th Corps with a dramatic eagle on the guard. Geary served as division commander in the 12th Corps defending Culp's Hill.

Sword of Union Gen. George Cobham, a brigade commander under Gen. John Geary. Cobham died at the battle of Peachtree Creek, Georgia, on July 20, 1864.

Wesley had often sported beneath the oaks of Culp's Hill, named after an extensive landowner of the period, Henry Culp." Wesley Culp visited his sisters and said he would return. He never did, as he died fighting on that hill and was buried there.

Many of the Union units fighting at Culp's Hill were from Pennsylvania and defending their home state. Brig.Gen. Thomas L. Kane led three regiments from the Keystone State, having hastened from a sick bed to be with his boys in one more fight. Kane survived the battle, but returned to his sick bed and died.

One more mighty clash of arms at Gettysburg remained: Lee's last supreme effort, the "Grand Assault," as J. Howard characterized Pickett's Charge. The stillness of the quiet afternoon along the front held by the Philadelphia Brigade was broken by about 150 Confederate cannons. Because the line of army Union Gen. Henry Hunt, in charge of Meade's artillery, could muster less than one hundred to return fire. "That third day's artillery at Gettysburg," J. Howard wrote:

> was the greatest and grandest of the Civil War. I shall attempt no description for it is one of those cases where the power of words is vain. While life lasts it can never pass from the memory of anyone who heard it. Oh! That withering tempest that swept over Cemetery Ridge from the converging fire of 150 cannon!

A Confederate religious flower horn used by Capt. McKim, who conducted religious prayers for Johnson's division at the Daniel Lady farm prior to attack on Culp's Hill.

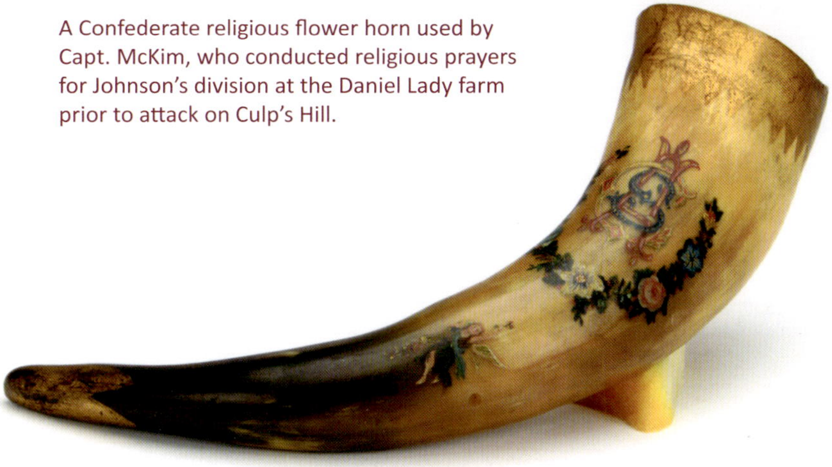

Sword and sash of Assistant Adjunct Benjamin Watkins Leigh of Confederate Gen. Edward Johnson's division. Johnson's troops fought at Culp's Hill. Leigh is said to have aided the mortally wounded Stonewall Jackson at Chancellorsville. Leigh's sash, pistol, pocket wallet, and a letter to him are shown. There are blood stains on the wallet.

Death and destruction of men and horses was horrible, and J. Howard wondered, "how any living were able to survive on the ridges swept by that orchestral tempest of death." J. Howard recorded that the barrage lasted one hour and fifty-five minutes and then suddenly ceased.

Next, from a fringe of woods a mile from the Union defenders, stepped out three battle lines of Confederate soldiers—a sublime spectacle. J. Howard called the action Longstreet's Grand Assault and Pickett's Charge. J. Howard described a gap in the Confederate march, Union Gen. Hancock's order that advanced Gen. George Stannard's Vermont brigades into the field, and the stopping of the Confederate's right and damaging of other Southern units. Union Gens. Hancock and Stannard were wounded in the action.

J. Howard was on the field that afternoon, taking reinforcing Union troops to their assigned locations. He described the gallant assault and the valiant defense. "In a moment all of the enemy were dead or wounded prisoners," J. Howard wrote of the final surge of Confederate Gen. Lewis Armistead and his men. "There were five minutes in which more history was written than any other five minutes of the ages. Those five minutes sealed the perpetuity of the Union, the death of slavery."

J. Howard proposed a rhetorical question in one of his writings about Gettysburg: "Is it necessary for Americans to go to Greece and Rome for exemplars of heroism?" J. Howard clearly believed the heroes of Gettysburg ranked equally with those of ancient times.

J. Howard's writing about Gettysburg and the Civil War drew praise from many of the leading participants of the conflict. His *Monuments and Indications of the Battle of Gettysburg* received acclaim from both sides of the war. Some of those who commented favorably on J. Howard's work included Gens. Sickles, Charles Graham, Howard, and Meade, and Cols. John Bachelder, George McFarland, Charles Banes, and Confederate Henry Kyd Douglass.

An English Kerr revolver, holster, and knife found at Pickett's Charge after the battle.

A pin with an "A"—a good luck item made from a San Francisco mint coin worn during prewar days—and a star from the collar worn by Gen. Lewis Armistead, who died after breaching the Union line during Pickett's Charge.

Items from Pickett's Charge include a Confederate haversack, bullets, a woman's photograph, a fork, a bullet mold, and a piece of hardtack (biscuit).

Significant Artifacts from the Gettysburg Battlefield

Leather map case of Maj. Jedediah Hotchkiss, noted topographic engineer of the Confederate Army. His maps are in the Library of Congress.

The commemorative first edition of the *Soldier's National Cemetery* printed in 1864.

A rare Confederate patriotic envelope, a locket with a woman's photograph, and a bullet found near where Confederate Gen. James Archer surrendered during the fighting on the first day.

Confederate Gen. Cadmus Wilcox's gold spurs given to Professor J. Howard Wert after the war.

Pennsylvania patriotic envelope with the hat insignia of Capt. R. Bruce Ricketts of the 1st Pennsylvania, 43rd Regiment battery, whose cannoneers gallantly fought on Cemetery Hill.

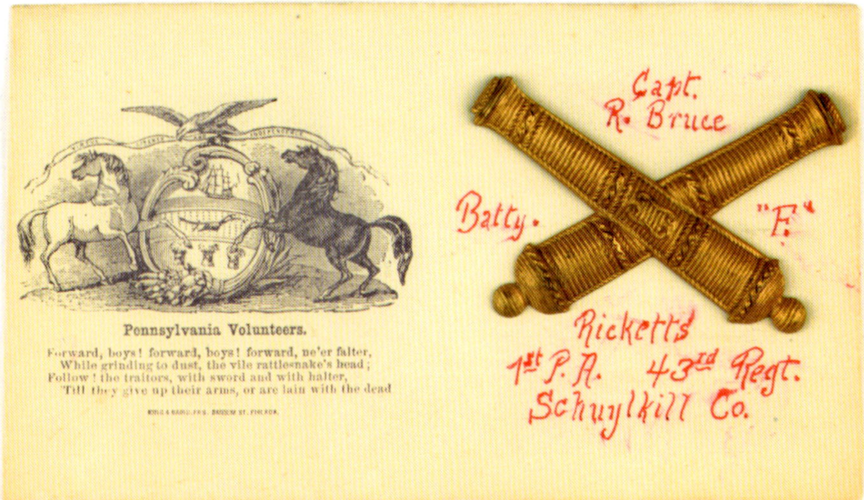

A horse bit, officer's whistle, and part of a saddle with the Crescent City insignia from the Washington Artillery of New Orleans from the grand cannonade on July 3, preceding Pickett's Charge.

A Currier and Ives depiction of Gen. Alexander Webb and the Philadelphia brigade defending Pickett's Charge.

Items from the command of Confederate Col. Thomas Henry Carter of the King William Artillery. His unit supported Pickett's Charge. Included are a box and spoon of Mordecai Kelly of the King William Artillery, a glass whiskey flask, a red folding wallet, and a base of a US shell fragment.

J. Howard Wert kept Union relics from the defensive line against Pickett's Charge in a wooden box, including a pouch, bullets, buttons, a belt buckle, and a Confederate cannon ball.

From Pickett's Charge: a Confederate pistol, a fragment of a rifle, an officer's sword tassel, shirt buttons, a tin container, and a knife.

Artifacts connected to Pickett's Charge from around the Codori Farm include a red Confederate belt and cap box, a flask, a red patent leather Bible, a Union shell fragment, a cartridge mold, and a master glass salt container.

Union artillery charges fired at Pickett's men, plus Confederate lead knuckles, part of a musket, and a bayonet found on the ground after the armies left Gettysburg.

A Confederate haversack and a Richmond round hardtack. A note by J. Howard Wert says, "Bread from dead Virginian's bag, Gettysburg July 5, 1863."

Gen. John Reynolds's camp hand fan with the insignia of First Corps.

Gen. John Reynolds's winter uniform frock coat.

From the area of Meade's headquarters on the Taneytown Road is a pewter flask belonging to Col. Addison Mason of Meade's staff, a white gauntlet, an ink well, and a staff officer's horse pistol.

Gen. John Reynolds's pre-Civil War formal dress chapeau.

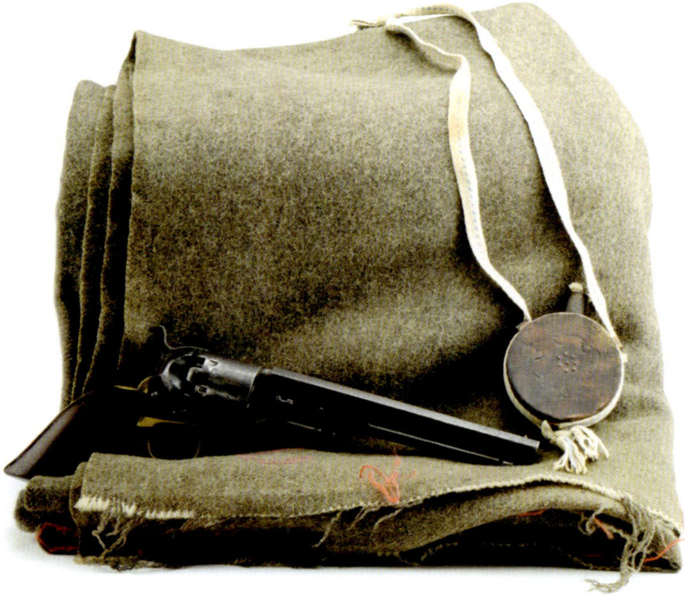

A Rebel blanket from Culp's Hill with an "S." sewn on it, as well as a miniature Rebel canteen and a Colt Navy 36 revolver from Culp's Hill.

Confederate John Gordon's saddle valise and silver tongs given to J. Howard Wert after the war by the general.

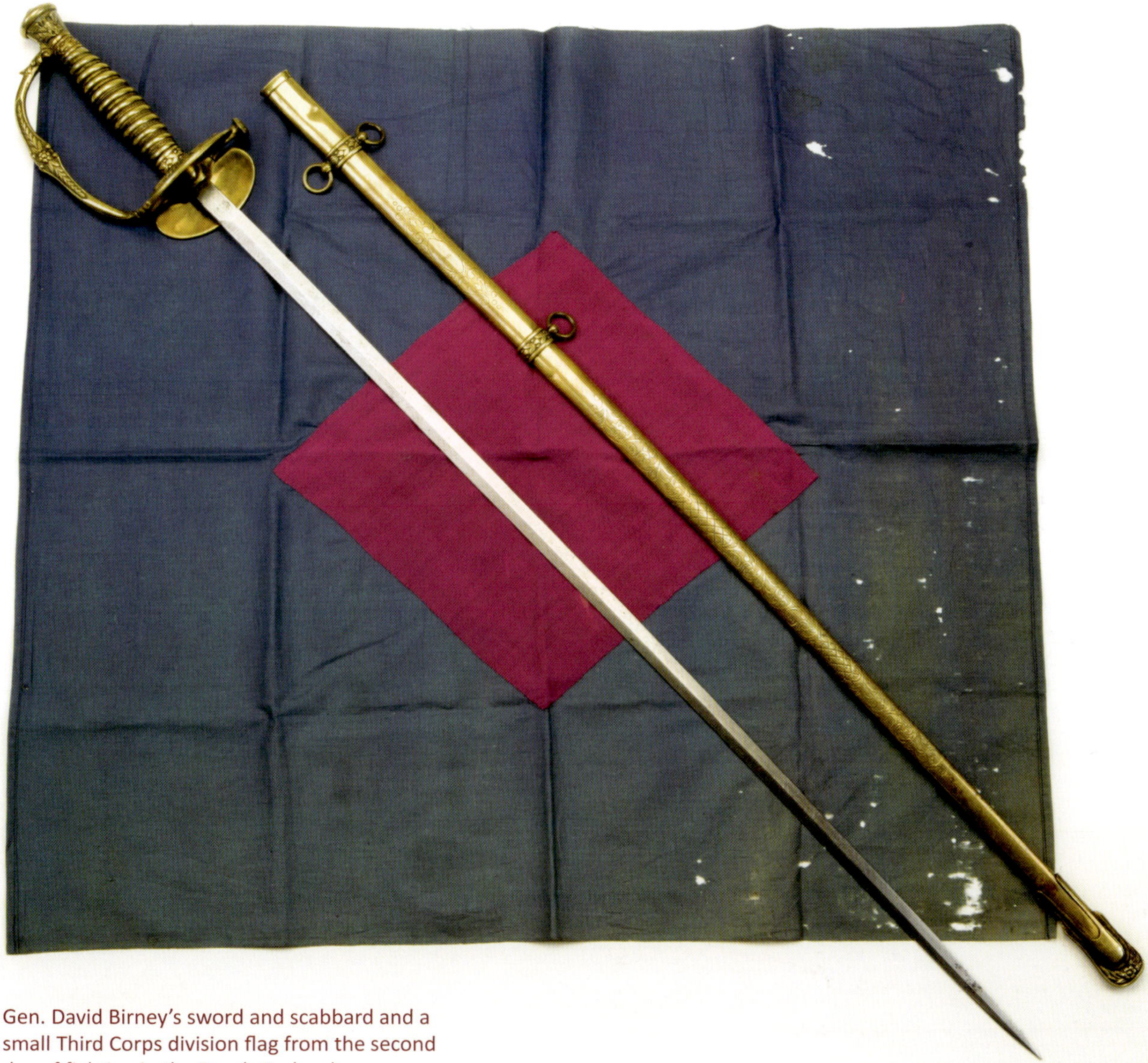

Gen. David Birney's sword and scabbard and a small Third Corps division flag from the second day of fighting in the Peach Orchard.

Artifacts of Lt. Col. Charles Mudge of the 2nd Massachusetts, who died in a charge near Culp's Hill on July 3.

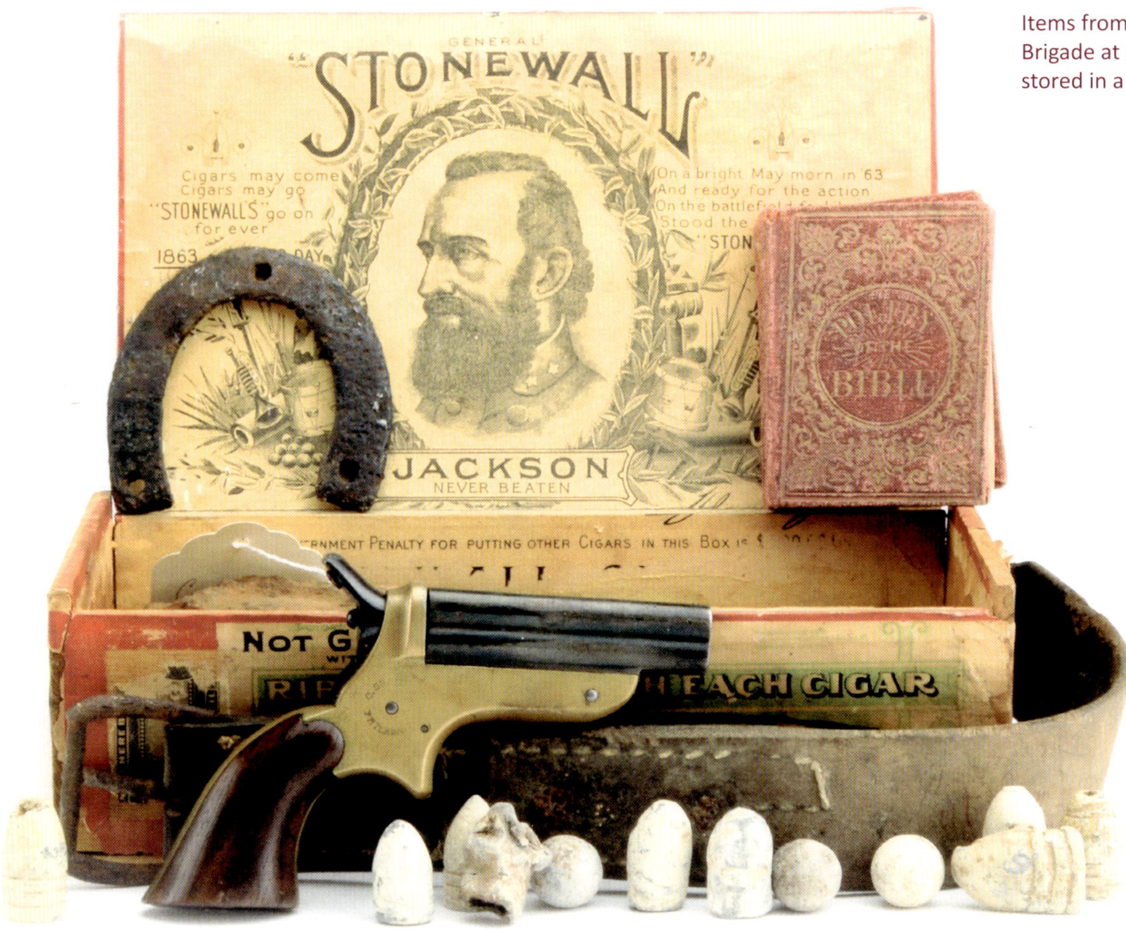

Items from the Stonewall Brigade at Culp's Hill were stored in a cigar box.

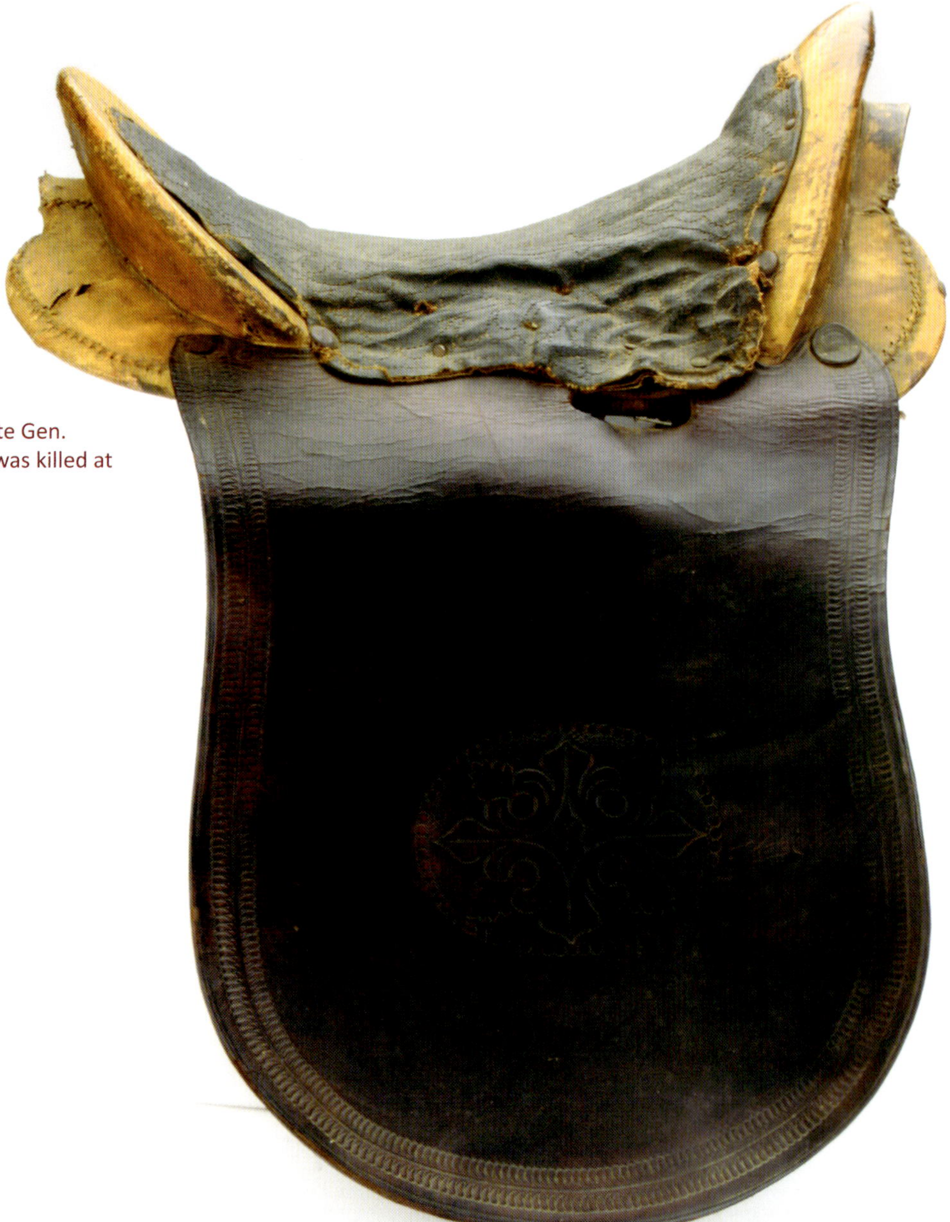

The saddle of Confederate Gen. William Barksdale, who was killed at Gettysburg.

Union Gen. Samuel Carroll of Maryland and his hat cord. Carroll helped defend against Pickett's Charge and also participated in the second day of the battle.

A note written by famed Kennett Square author Bayard Taylor and a "buck tail pipe belonging to Col. Charles Taylor, Bayard's brother, who was killed at Gettysburg on the second day of fighting. Charles was twenty-three when he died and a member of the 13th Pennsylvania.

Rare Confederate oil cloth kepi found at the Lutheran Seminary.

Chapter Five

GETTYSBURG'S AFTERMATH

After the battle of Gettysburg nine white-walled hospital cities stretching over meadows and forests held more than 20,000 wounded soldiers of both armies. At first every house and barn for many miles was a hospital from which came day and night, without cessation, shrieks of agony and the gurgle of death. The amputation tables, with a never-ending round of occupants, stood in cornfields, at the doors of abandoned churches, and in the orchards of devastated farms.

An article J. Howard wrote for the *Gettysburg Compiler* printed on January 8, 1908, described the town. He wrote:

> After that bloody First of July, 1863, at Gettysburg the little town was rapidly filled to its utmost capacity with shattered and shot-torn men. All the churches, school buildings, warehouses, halls and public edifices were crowded with the wounded who lay in long rows on the floors or on trestles hastily constructed with boards from adjacent lumber yards. They were in tailor shops, doctors' offices, coach factories, dismantled groceries, photographers' rooms, print shops, smithies, everywhere.
>
> But there was a vast overflow that was taken into private houses. Nearly every dwelling sheltered some of the sufferers. Many had as high as fifteen or twenty of the heroes of the Army of the Potomac; some as many as forty or fifty.

J. Howard wrote in later newspaper articles for the *Harrisburg Telegraph* about the hospitals of Gettysburg, about the "saddest and most pathetic sight in all of the universes." J. Howard continued:

> When the splender, the pomp and the circumstance of battles' magnificently stern array have gone, then the horrible and the ghastly remain in their most terrible forms. Hideous is the sorrowful appearance of the bloated, distorted and blackened dead, so

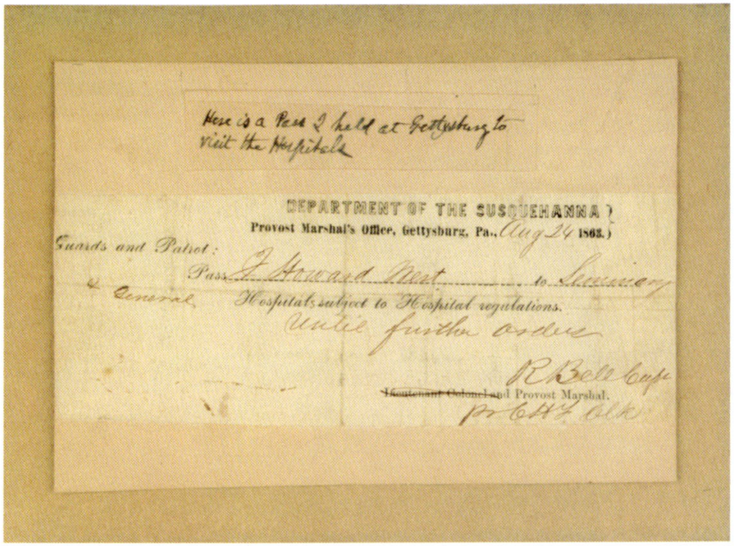

Here is a Pass I held at Gettysburg to visit the Hospitals

DEPARTMENT OF THE SUSQUEHANNA
Provost Marshal's Office, Gettysburg, Pa., Aug 24 1863.

Guards and Patrol:
Pass J. Howard Wert to Seminary & General Hospitals subject to Hospital regulations.
Until further orders

R Bell Capt
~~Lieutenant Colonel~~ and Provost Marshal.
pr C H F Clk

J. Howard Wert's pass to visit Gettysburg hospitals issued on August 24, 1863.

> lately noble, stalwart men, as they are packed together, side by side, some in blue and some in gray.

The hospitals were described by J. Howard as being filled with the horrible agony of the wounded and where "speedy death often would be in an unspeakable boon." Wounded waited days before being brought to hospitals for treatment, and the dead were also delayed being interred. Thousands of the wounded were Southerners left on the field and thousands of others captured by the Union army, according to J. Howard in the Harrisburg newspaper:

> Immediately after the battle every church and school building, every hall and warehouse in the town of Gettysburg, every barn for miles around in every direction was a hospital. The theological seminary crowded with mourners moaning a life away. Other men, shot out of all semblance to humanity, were nursed and cared for by tender hands in nearly every glowing house in town and country. Others, less seriously wounded, looked out for themselves.

> The hospitals' locations were detailed by J. Howard:

> Those of the 11th and 12th corps were west of Rock Creek on the extensive George Bushman farm and other contiguous properties. All of the others were east of the stream and generally quite near Rock Creek or its affluents. The central point of the Second Corps hospital was on the Moses Schwartz farm but it lapped over lands of the adjacent properties. This was by far the largest of the field hospitals; … the Southern warriors, were by thousands in the hospital of this corp. It contained a greater number of them than all other field hospitals combined. In some cases the space devoted to a single regiment, as in the case of the 64th New York, would have appeared as a large hospital on many battlefields. South of the 2nd Corps, which reached to the banks of White Run began the hospital of Sickles' 3rd Corps, running through thick forest and along the bluffs of Rock Creek, White Run and the Two Taverns Run, it occupied not only the large farm of Michael Fiscel, but lapped over on several contiguous properties.

To the south and east of 3rd Corps hospital was one devoted to the 5th Corps. One division was devoted to Pennsylvania reserves, including some soldiers from Gettysburg, and Ayres' regulars. This hospital, bordering at one point on Two Taverns Run, extended either side of the public road through long stretches of forest, and a short distance east of its termination began the farms occupied by the suffering men of Gen. John Reynolds's 1st Corps. The location was along the Baltimore Pike, close to the Union position on Cemetery Hill. Three encampments were close to the Wert home. The first division was at the historic white-framed church known as Mark's Church in memory of J. Howard's great-grandfather, who donated the land and was instrumental in erecting the church almost a century before it was "filled with the shot-shattered men who had stayed Hill's advance on the first day of the battle," noted J. Howard.

The second and third divisions of the 1st Corps were on the farms of Sheriff Isaac Lightner and Peter Conover. The cavalry hospitals were scattered over the hills, barns, and fields where Union Gen. Gregg and Confederate Gen. J. E. B. Stuart's cavalry units fought. "After many weeks the field hospitals were gradually depleted and thousands, as they recovered sufficiently to endure railway travel, were sent to their homes or forwarded to city hospitals in Harrisburg, Philadelphia, New York and Baltimore," J. Howard wrote. "The other cause of the depletion was mournfully told by the long trenches in the wheat fields and meadows with newly turned ground. In this, side-by-side, wrapped only in a blanket or encased in a coffin of rude construction were long rows of the blue and the gray who had fought their last battle."

The aftermath of the battle completely absorbed the Wert family. Family members tended to the wounded soldiers from North and South, in keeping with its Christian faith. Aunt Katie, J. Howard's mother, was often seen praying for the soldiers as she helped nurse them back to health at field hospitals and at Camp Letterman, just east of Gettysburg. J. Howard was also a constant visitor in the many hospitals along the Baltimore Pike and later at Camp Letterman.

The Wert family joined many Gettysburg residents in offering assistance. In a *Gettysburg Compiler* article of January 8, 1908, J. Howard wrote:

> The kindness of the good people of Gettysburg, as far as their scanty means permitted, was inexhaustible. In all this noble work the women were foremost. Most of the tales of women's devotion and heroism during those dark days have passed into oblivion, as the angels of mercy

A demijohn bottle for spirits used in the Gettysburg hospitals.

> themselves and the recipients of their labors of love have alike passed through the shadowy valley.

J. Howard detailed the story of a young wounded soldier, George Engle of Company C of the 143rd Pennsylvania. Engle made his way to a Catholic church on High Street, but the church was full of wounded soldiers. Jane Powers, a daughter of Solomon Powers, and another young Gettysburg woman, Lizzie Sweeney, were at the church, and they took Engle back to the Powers home at the corner of Washington and High streets.

The Powers's home had at least fifteen wounded soldiers when Engle arrived. The women tended to the wounds and prepared meals from the meager supply of food remaining in the home. Food was scarce throughout the Gettysburg area. J. Howard noted:

> In the eyes of these noble women each man that wore the blue was a hero, no matter what his nationality or how lowly his rank in life. In the eyes of these pain-racked men each one of these indefatigable nurses was something very near akin to a goddess.

Vermont Bennington Pottery figurine mug owned by Gettysburg stonecutter Solomon Powers, who hailed from Vermont, and a decorative tin box. The Powers parents and girls did gallant service in the hospitals caring for the wounded.

J. Howard took on a number of tasks, including writing and distributing stories to newspapers about the battle and helping grieving relatives of fallen soldiers find the graves of their loved ones. Exhuming the soldiers and preparing their bodies for transportation were trying and tragic experiences for family members.

Annie Roberts of Brooklyn, New York, was one such relative helped by J. Howard. Her brother and husband fought with the 14th New York, known as the 14th Brooklyn. After the battle she came to Gettysburg looking for her relatives. Despite being denied access to Gettysburg by Union officials, she made her way to the scene of the battle, was one of the first civilians to visit the battlefield, and met J. Howard. She visited many of the hospitals searching for her husband and brother. J. Howard guided her over the ground of the first day's battle and they found artifacts from the 14th New York. Many of the soldiers from the unit had been buried in common graves.

Roberts found the body of her brother with one of his legs missing. Her husband, she discovered later, had been taken prisoner by the Confederates and was held at Libby Prison in Richmond. J. Howard wrote that Annie's story was one of many that played out on the fields of Gettysburg:

> At Gettysburg the dead of both armies, as a general rule, were interred with as much care as circumstances would permit. Yet at the best, the burials of the battlefield must seem shocking and sacrilegious as compared with the respect paid to the dead in our own homes.

In Plum Run, near Devil's Den, the bodies of five Confederate soldiers were discovered a month after the battle. They were piled upon each other just as they had fallen. "It was a hideous and revolting spectacle," J. Howard wrote:

> but war is replete with horrors. Whenever the writer views these rocks around the Devil's Den, where so many brave men yielded up life, his mind reverts to a black-haired, handsome youth of an Alabama regiment who, after the battle, lay for weeks in the hospital of the Second Army Corps, moaning with pain. Much of the time he was partially delirious from the fever and suffering induced by his shattered leg. The amputation of which had been too long delayed. In all his ravings the prominent subject was those, "Awful, awful rocks." He had fallen near this point and those weird surroundings, so different from his Southern home, were ever foremost in his mind and through all of the weeks of suffering, till death came.

J. Howard visited Culp's Hill before any of the Confederates were buried, and on the sloping hillside and a ravine he said he saw the dead more thickly strewn than on any other part of the battlefield. At the scene of a charge J. Howard recorded seeing three or four bodies piled one upon the other. The burials on Culp's Hill were more thorough than upon any other part of the field. Deep, long trenches were dug, and from twelve to seventy-three bodies were placed in each one. Soldiers would then record on a section of bark the number buried in each trench. There were seventeen trenches in a space of less than six acres.

In the Evergreen Cemetery in Gettysburg the battle damaged a grave marker of a young girl. A white marble lamb was found on top of a gun carriage, recorded Lt. Frank Haskell of Gen. John Gibbons's staff. The grave marker was repaired that same year by stone cutter Soloman Powers. Eventually the marker needed to be replaced and the original white marble lamb was given to J. Howard for his collection.

While in Evergreen Cemetery, just days after the battle J. Howard came across the grave of his childhood friend, Fred Huber. The two went to Pennsylvania College and were members of the Black Ducks before Huber joined the 23rd Pennsylvania. Huber was killed at the Battle of Fair Oaks and his body was returned to Gettysburg. On the grave was a photograph of a young girl holding flowers. The girl was never identified. The photograph is in the Wert collection.

Lamb headstone for a young girl that was damaged in the Evergreen Cemetery, Gettysburg. The lamb was found on top of a gun carriage and later repaired by Gettysburg stonecutter Solomon Powers. Upon replacement years after the war the original lamb headstone was given to J. Howard Wert for his collection.

The non-com sword of J. Howard Wert's childhood friend, Fred Huber. They went to Pennsylvania College and were members of the Black Ducks. Huber joined the 23rd Pennsylvania and was killed at the Battle of Fair Oaks. He was subsequently buried at Evergreen Cemetery, only to have the battle of Gettysburg severely damage his tombstone, so a piece was labeled and wrapped in black silk, then attached to his sword.

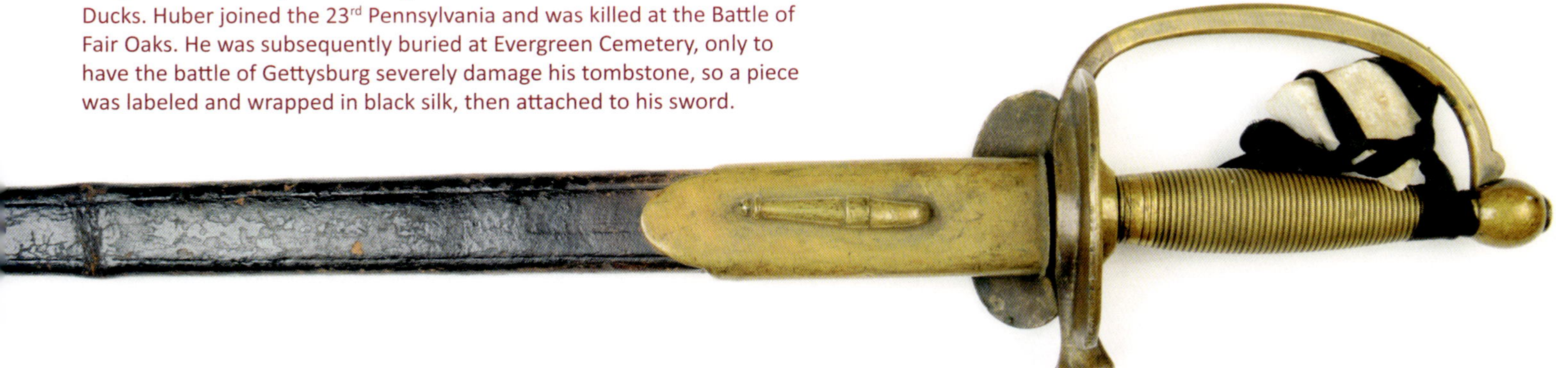

J. Howard also rode on the battlefield two days after the battle with Haskell. Haskell wrote about the battle in the days following Gettysburg. "As we rode about the battlefield seeing the carnage, Frank and I discussed the battle scenes in a solemn manner," J. Howard later told his grandson, Bernard Wert. Haskell and J. Howard rode their horses from the Wert farm to Baltimore Pike and on toward Gettysburg, Bernard Wert said. During that ride the two soldiers discussed what they saw on the battlefield and the aftermath that affected Gettysburg for decades.

Granddaughter Margaret Wert confirmed that the Haskell family gave her grandfather a cased photograph and a small pair of silver spurs. A heel spike was very distinctive, according to Margaret Wert.

Margaret Wert said her grandfather often recalled that Union generals lavished praise on Haskell's heroic role at Gettysburg. Gen. Francis A. Walker wrote that Haskell was:

> one who was bravest of the brave, riding mounted through an interval between the Union battalions and calling upon the troops to go forward. . . [Haskell] called upon the men of the Second Division to follow him and setting an example of valor and self-devotion never forgotten by any man of the thousands who witnessed it."

In his official reports Gen. John Gibbon called "particular attention to the manner in which several subordinate reports mention the services of my gallant aide, Lieutenant F. A. Haskell." Gen. Winfield Scott Hancock also singled out Haskell for praise in his report.

Haskell and J. Howard saw many wounded soldiers from both armies, as fields in J. Howard's neighborhood became one vast hospital. Many badly wounded soldiers were brought to a building along Taneytown Road, where many died and were buried. At every house, barn, shed, and cooling brook Haskell saw wounded. Haskell wrote, "They were members of a great army, a mutilated, bruised mass of humanity." The men suffered

Col. Frank Haskell's Dartmouth College graduation portrait, his spurs, and a first edition of his book on the battle of Gettysburg.

from every type of wound "that iron and lead can make, blunt or sharp, bullet, ball, and shell, piercing, bruising, tearing was there. . . ."

J. Howard also wrote about the scene, recording:

> Everywhere were festering corpses. Many were still unburied; other dead had been rudely and hastily interred with so little earth upon them that the appearance presented was almost as repulsive as where no attempt at burial had been made. In some cases nothing but a few mutilated fragments and pieces of flesh could be seen of what had been so lately a human being following his flag to death or victory. As one went from the Wheatfield along the remainder of the battle line of July 2nd, everywhere, in fact, were the same mute, sorrowful memorials of a sad fraternal slaughter.

The doctors were also described by Haskell following the repulse of Pickett's Charge:

> The surgeons, with coats off and sleeves rolled-up and the hospital attendants with green bands upon their caps are about their work and their faces and clothes are splattered with blood and though they look weary and tired, their work goes systematically and steadily on. How much and how long they have worked, the piles of legs, arms, feet, hands, and fingers about partially tell. . . . Nearby appear a row of small fresh mounds, placed side by side. They were not there before yesterday. They will become more numerous every day.

Haskell was looking for Gibbon and found him sitting on a chair, having his wounded left shoulder bathed in cold water. Hancock, wounded during the third day's fighting at Pickett's Charge, was in an ambulance. Both men were at the Second Corps hospital on Rock Run Creek. Gibbon greeted Haskell and shook his hand. Gibbon believed he was wounded near a spot where he watched the beginning of cannonade on July 3.

Since Gibbon was wounded before the repulse of Pickett's Charge he asked Haskell to describe the climax of the Gettysburg battle. The focal point of the attack was the section of the wall defended by Gen. Alexander Webb and the Philadelphia brigade. Soldiers gathered around Haskell as he described the action. "I never had so enthusiastic an audience before," he wrote. "Cries

A Philadelphia woman, Emily Sauders, helped at the 2nd Corps hospital at Gettysburg and wrote a book. Shown are Sauders's hospital prayer book, wallet, and a Rebel bullet.

Medical bag and contents used at the First Corps hospital at Mark's Church, Gettysburg. The bag was made in Philadelphia by John E. Maris of South Third Street, Philadelphia.

Gen. Winfield Scott Hancock's photograph and saddle blanket eagle.

of 'good,' 'glorious,' frequently interrupted me and the storming of the wall was applauded by enthusiastic tears and the waving of battered and bloody hands."

Haskell accompanied Gibbon to Westminister—the closest operating train station—and saw Gibbon transferred from an ambulance to the train for a trip to Baltimore on July 4. Haskell then returned to the battlefield under the command of Gen. William Harrow. Two days later he rode the battlefield with J. Howard.

The two men went to the field where the battle began on July 1. They could tell where the battle raged:

> discarded and splintered muskets, rent knapsacks and haversacks, bruised canteens, shreds of caps, coats, trousers of blue or gray cloth, worthless belts and cartridge boxes, torn blankets, ammunition boxes, broken wheels, smashed limbers, shattered gun carriages, parts of harness, of all that men or horse wear or use in battle were scattered over miles of the field.

J. Howard noted the effect of the heavy rain that fell on July 4, the day after the fighting at Gettysburg concluded:

> After the ground had been settled by a heavy rain, appeared shoes and hats, locks of hair and portions of the bodies. Oh! The sorrowful appearance of those bloated, distorted, and blackened dead as they lay scattered over the field of battle. Noble, stalwart men were they, arrayed in garb of gray, or blue, who had fought bravely—desperately. A battle has never been described by the most brilliant writer so as to give the reader a full conception of its intensity of both splendor and horror.

Salvageable equipment was gathered by the Union army and civilians were told that such equipment was property of the army. The warning did not deter men, boys, and girls from loitering about the field, looking for mementoes to keep. Haskell said they especially looked for workable muskets and untorn blankets so they could make a profit. He wrote that men were charged a dollar by some civilians for a small strip of old linen to bind their wounds.

At Seminary Ridge, where the Confederates' attack formed for Pickett's Charge, the two soldiers (J. Howard and Haskell) saw evidence of the accuracy of the Union artillery fire. Trees were destroyed by shells and Confederate graves were visible. "Upon a single tree, not over a foot and a half in diameter, I actually counted as many as two hundred and fifty bullet marks," Haskell wrote. Similar evidence was found at Culp's Hill, where Confederates tried to dislodge Union troops holding the army's right flank on the final two days of fighting. J. Howard and Haskell noticed newly dug graves on Culp's Hill with notes written in red chalk stating the number of Confederates buried in the trenches. One read, "75 Rebels buried here." The Union soldiers were buried in graves and placed at the head were the name and regiment of the dead soldier.

Haskell wrote that he would have liked to have seen a more formal burial of the Rebel troops, but circumstances would not allow such burials. He also noted that Union dead on the first day were stripped of their clothing and left naked in the sun until being buried after the battle.

Gettysburg the town did not escape damage. Haskell and J. Howard saw about every public building and private home was used to nurse wounded soldiers. Riding through the streets J. Howard saw signs of bullets splattering fences and walls, and shells had riddled some of the houses, making holes through all of the walls. Despite orders from Confederate officers warning not to plunder, Rebels had taken drugs, medicines, clothing, tin ware, and groceries without compensation. Libraries, both public and private, had been entered and books scattered about in yards or destroyed, according to Haskell's description.

A great number of private dwellings had been occupied during the battle and wantonly destroyed. Furniture had been smashed, beds ripped open, and civilians robbed of money, watches, and jewelry.

Found on Culp's Hill was a handmade Confederate pouch and a section of wood torn from a tree with part of a projectile.

The grave marker of a soldier from the 26th North Carolina. Square nail holes can be seen that were common in the Civil War era.

J. Howard said his July 6, 1863, ride with Haskell also impressed upon him the value of the battle's historical evidence and the need to collect artifacts, according to Margaret Wert. J. Howard wrote, "The people of the past, who saw and experienced the war, are represented years hence by their memories and their memorabilia." Also, J. Howard told family members that many of the conversations he had with Haskell that day were included in Haskell's book on Gettysburg. J. Howard wrote in one of his books:

> The writer of the history was over the Wheatfield and the adjacent battle line, July 6, 1863, and many subsequent days of that month. No words can portray the awful picture of desolation, devastation, and death presented. Fences and fruits of the earth had alike disappeared before the withering besom of destruction. All was a trodden, miry waste, with corpses at every step, and the thickly littered debris of battle—broken muskets and soiled bayonets, shattered ammunition chests and blood defiled clothing, trodden cartridge boxes and splintered swords, rifled knapsacks and battered canteens.

Even though J. Howard and Haskell did their best to describe the battle and the aftermath of Gettysburg, Wert knew that words could not tell the whole story:

> It must be seen and experienced to be understood. But if the most skilled of word painters have failed to depict the field of conflict when the passionate strife has ceased—when the splendor, the pomp, and the circumstances of battle's magnificently stern array have gone, and only the horrible remains in the ghastliest and most terrible forms.

Less than a year after J. Howard rode the battle with Haskell, on June 3, 1864, Haskell was killed at the Battle of Cold Harbor. A Confederate sharpshooter ended Haskell's life.

The nation knew immediately that the Gettysburg scenes described by J. Howard and Haskell and the tremendous sacrifices made by Americans had to be commemorated.

The days of the Gettysburg campaign were anxious ones for President Abraham Lincoln. Navy Secretary Gideon Wells reported in his diary finding Lincoln at the War Department on July 2 reading dispatches from Gen. George Meade. Telegraph operator Homer Bates reported Lincoln was in the office, "hour after hour during those anxious days and nights." On the final day of fighting at Gettysburg Lincoln again was at the War Department with Wells and Secretary of State William Seward, examining dispatches from Meade, even though he must have been distracted by reports of Mary Lincoln receiving a head injury when she was thrown from a carriage during a drive to the Soldiers' Home.

On the morning of Saturday, July 4, 1863, Lincoln issued a press release, saying the Army of the Potomac had covered itself with the highest honor. The next day Lincoln and his son Tad visited Gen. Dan Sickles, who was transported to Washington after his leg amputation in Gettysburg.

By July 6, Lincoln was concerned Meade was not aggressively pursuing the retreating Confederate army. Union Gen. Herman Haupt reported to Lincoln that Gen. Robert E. Lee's army was escaping. Lincoln asked Gen. Henry Halleck, "Does General Meade intend to cover Baltimore and Washington, and get enemy across river again without further collision, or does he plan to

Cuff buttons made into earrings given to Emma Aughinbaugh Wert by Gen. Dan Sickles.

prevent his crossing and to destroy him?" On July 7, Wells reported that Lincoln appeared despondent because Meade had lingered at Gettysburg. Lincoln wrote to Adj. Gen. Lorenzo Thomas that Meade's troops would be of "no imaginable service" if they did not move with more speed. He concluded his message by saying Meade's army, "will, in my unprofessional opinion, be quite as likely to capture the Man-in-the Moon, as any part of Lee's Army." When Lincoln received a message on July 12 of Meade's plan to attack Lee, Lincoln muttered "too late," according to Bates in the telegraph office.

In November 1863, President Lincoln prepared for his visit to Gettysburg to deliver what became the Gettysburg Address. J. Howard witnessed and recorded the visit of Lincoln and the delivery of the Gettysburg Address on Thursday, November 19, 1863. In fact, J. Howard was a marshal designated by Pennsylvania College during the delivery of the historic speech and stood in front of Lincoln. He wore a white sash and a hat with ear flaps during the address. Haskell was also present during the giving of the address, along with Gen. Gibbon.

The presidential train arrived in Gettysburg on Wednesday evening. The next morning ceremonies began for the dedication of the National Cemetery, with Maj. Gen. Darius Couch in charge. J. Howard wrote the line of parade was taken up at 10:00 a.m., and proceeded through town streets to the cemetery, where the military formed in line and saluted President Lincoln.

The program was organized by David Wills of Gettysburg and a committee he formed. Wills hosted President Lincoln during the visit. The program included:

Music by Birgfeld's Band, *Homage d'uns Heros* by Adolph Birgfeld
Prayer by Reverend T. H. Stockton, D.D.
Music by the Marine Band, *Old Hundred*, directed by Francis Scala
Oration by Hon. Edward Everett, *The Battles of Gettysburg*
Music hymn *Consecration Chant* by B. B. French, Esq., music by Wilson G. Horner, sung by Baltimore Glee Club
Dedicatory Remarks by the President of the United States
Dirge *Oh! It is Great for Our Country to Die*, words by James G. Percival, music by Alfred Delaney and sung by choir selected for the occasion
Benediction by Reverend H. L. Baugher, D.D.

According to J. Howard, at a quarter past 11:00 a.m. the head of the procession arrived at the main stand: "President Lincoln, cabinet members, military and civilian dignitaries were on the stand with Lincoln seated between Messars [William] Seward and [Edward] Everett," Wert recorded:

> After a moment of silence, with every man among the immense gathering uncovering on his appearance. The

J. Howard Wert's college song book from 1860 and the sash and hat he wore during the Gettysburg Address. Wert was a graduate of Pennsylvania College and was a college marshal during Lincoln's Gettysburg Address parade in November 1863.

Handbill distributed in Gettysburg of President Lincoln's election in 1860.

Henry L. Baugher, president of Pennsylvania College 1850–1868, spoke after President Lincoln gave his Gettysburg Address on November 19, 1863. Shown is Baugher and his reading glasses.

A shawl, stick pin, and locket worn by Gettysburg teenager Tillie Pierce at the Gettysburg Address. Pierce was a friend of Wert and wrote *At Gettysburg: What a Girl Saw and Heard of the Battle*.

Book, glasses, photograph, and a case belonging to Pennsylvania College Professor Michael Jacobs. Jacobs was a friend of J. Howard Wert, and he also owned the podium used by President Lincoln during the Gettysburg Address. The 1864 book by Lippincott, *Rebel Invasion of Maryland & Pennsylvania and Battle of Gettysburg*, contains one of the first maps of the battlefield.

> military then formed in line, extending around the area, the rest of the space being occupied by civilians comprising about 15,000 people and including men, women and children. The attendance of ladies was quite large.
>
> The military escort comprised one squadron of cavalry, two batteries of artillery and a regiment of infantry, being the regular funeral escort of honor paid to the highest officers of the service. After the performance of the funeral military dirge by Birgfeld's band, an eloquent prayer was delivered by Reverend [Stockton].
>
> Mr. Everett then commenced the delivery of his oration which was listened to with marked attention throughout. . . . Numerous flags and banners suitably draped were exhibited on the stand and among the audience. The entire scene was one of grandeur due to the importance of the occasion.
>
> The President then delivered the following dedicatory speech: . . .three cheers were then given for the President of the United States and governors of the states. After the delivery of the address the dirge and benediction closed the exercises and the immense assemblage separated about two o'clock.
>
> The President's party started for Washington at 6 o'clock this evening followed by the governors' trains. Thousands of people were gathered at the depot anxiously awaiting transportation to their homes but they will probably be confined to the meager accommodations of Gettysburg till tomorrow.

After the Gettysburg Address J. Howard's life changed, as in 1864, he enlisted in the 209th Pennsylvania Volunteers as a lieutenant. He fought with the armies of the Potomac and James. His unit was recruited in a number of Pennsylvania counties, including Adams, York, Cambria, Franklin, Columbia, Cumberland, Lehigh, and Lebanon. Company G came from Adams County. They enlisted for a year.

The 209th was formally organized at Camp Curtin, Harrisburg, on September 16, 1864, and left for Bermuda Hundred, Virginia, the next day. The officers were Col. Tobias B. Kauffman, Lt. Col. George W. Frederick, and Maj. John L. Ritchey.

J. Howard and his comrades stayed with the Army of the James until November. The unit was placed at Camp Potter, near Petersburg, Virginia, where it remained for two weeks before being posted upon the advance line to the left of Fort Harrison, midway between the James and Appomattox Rivers. The 209th

J. Howard Wert's framed memorial from his unit, the 209th Pennsylvania.

Pennsylvania took part in the capture of Fort Harrison. On November 17, 1864, the Confederates attacked the unit's picket line and Capt. Henry Lee, Lt. Thomas J. Hendricks, and nineteen enlisted men were captured. One member of the unit was killed and two were wounded.

A week later the regiment and other Pennsylvania regiments were transferred to the Army of the Potomac and assigned to Ninth Army Corps. The 209th joined the 200th and 208th Pennsylvania regiments, forming the First Brigade under Col. Charles W. Diven. For a month they were in Gen. John Hartranft's Provisional Brigade. They remained assigned to the First Brigade, Third Division, Ninth Army Corps for the rest of the war.

The 209th Pennsylvania took part in the heavy fighting at Fort Steadman, where Lt. Hugh Jones, commanding Company C, was shot in the head and died. The unit was part of the troops entering Petersburg, Virginia, when the Confederates abandoned the city. The regiment was then ordered to Nottoway Court House.

In all, the 209th Pennsylvania was involved in a number of actions, including siege operations against Petersburg and Richmond, Dabney's Mills, Hatcher's Run, and Fort Stedman. They were at Nottoway Court House April 9–20, 1865, and the unit then went to City Point and Alexandria. They participated in the Grand Review of Union troops through the streets of Washington, DC, on May 23–24, 1865, and were mustered out of service on May 31, 1865.

During the war the regiment lost two officers and seventeen enlisted men killed and mortally wounded, and twenty enlisted men by disease.

Chapter Six

WERT FAMILY COLLECTION

The Wert family collection is one of the oldest collections of Americana with an emphasis on Gettysburg, documented as dating to 1711. The collection dates to Capt. Jacob Wert. He saved items from the American Revolution. His son, Jacob Wert Jr., high constable of Gettysburg, continued adding to the collection during the Federal era.

Adam Wert did not believe in discarding items and J. Howard was raised in the same tradition. J. Howard established the family motto: "Preserve for Prosperity."

The main bulk of the collection came from the Civil War and Gettysburg. The serious collection began in the days following the battle, while the Wert family was engaged in caring for wounded soldiers and helping the families of the deceased. Adam Wert encouraged his son J. Howard to preserve mementos given to him or found on the battlefield. J. Howard gathered items that were discarded, lost, or abandoned in the days following the battle.

Thus, J. Howard began gathering relics as symbols of military valor and mementos reflecting a new birth of freedom. Robert Swift wrote in *Gettysburg* magazine, "J. Howard Wert never lost his passion for the causes of his youth. That passion led Wert to become one of the great keepers of the flame of the nineteenth century movement to abolish slavery and the war to preserve the Union."

In a way, the collection provides a look into J. Howard's childhood and heritage. He was told the stories of family members taking part in major events of the nation's history, including the French and Indian War, the American Revolution, and the War of 1812.

After the Civil War J. Howard returned to teaching and became superintendent of Adams County schools. A decade after the battle J. Howard was one of the local leaders of the Grand Army of the Republic (GAR), a fraternal organization composed of veterans of the Union army and navy who served in the Civil War.

J. Howard was inspired by his friend, John Bachelder, in a project of publishing a book in the 1870s. J. Howard's book on the monuments of the battlefield came out in 1886. Bachelder favorably commented on J. Howard's work. Bachelder had studied the terrain of the battlefield and drew isometric

Silver pistol and side knife belonging to Wilhelm Houghtelin. The pistol was made in England and was used in the American Revolution, including the Battle of Brandywine on September 11, 1777.

maps. J. Howard visited field hospitals, interviewed wounded soldiers of both armies, and later interviewed officers of both armies.

Bachelder also served on the Gettysburg Battlefield Memorial Association. In 1880, President Rutherford B. Hayes, a Civil War veteran, signed into law a bill which provided Bachelder $50,000 to write a detailed history of the battle. The major work on the battle never materialized.

J. Howard's fellow veterans and Civil War comrades that gave him objects appreciated the fact J. Howard wanted the items to be preserved for posterity. J. Howard became a nationally recognized expert on Gettysburg and his three-story, fashionable townhouse in Harrisburg near the capitol building became a repository for Gettysburg relics. Many notable Union officers donated items, including Gen. Dan Sickles, Maj. John Bigelow, and Gen. Charles K. Graham, who was wounded in the hip while fighting at the Peach Orchard on July 2, and was captured by the Confederates. Graham was later exchanged for Confederate Gen. James L. Kemper in September 1863. Kemper was seriously wounded in Pickett's Charge at Gettysburg and was later captured by the Union.

Not only was J. Howard recognized as an authority on the battle of Gettysburg, but his collection became nationally known. On March 27, 1910, the *New York Herald* noted:

> Probably the rarest and most valuable private collection of war relics from the battlefields of the Civil War is that owned by Professor J. Howard Wert. Gettysburg was his home and he was there during the great decisive battle, acting as a guide to the Union forces and doing other patriotic work.

The *New York Herald* also credited J. Howard for documenting the artifacts as to where they were recovered from the battlefield

A pocket lance set belonging to Benjamin Rush, signer of the Declaration of Independence.

A leather bag and case belonging to Confederate Gen. James Kemper and a copy of the song *Auld Lang Syne* favored by Freemasons. Kemper was a Mason and served as governor of Virgnia.

A pistol, cartridge box, haversack, blackjack, and a dirk dagger belonging to the Louisiana Tigers from their charge on Cemetery Hill.

and who owned them when possible. "There are many things that are seldom found in similar collections," the article stated. In 1984, a *Time-Life* article by Brian Pohanka about Gettysburg added:

> While fighting still raged near his family's farmhouse, a young school teacher and writer named J. Howard Wert began to gather up what he called "the thickly littered debris of battle." Wert returned often to the ravaged field selecting and carefully identifying items from the debris with a keen eye for the memorable and the poignant.

Granddaughter Margaret Wert said after the *New York Herald* article was published many donations were given to her grandfather by fellow veterans. Margaret added that after J. Howard published a book he would receive additional artifacts from soldiers and statesmen. She said his participation in GAR also spurred donations from veterans. Margaret said her grandfather prized all of his keepsakes, but since he rode with the heroic Lt. Frank Haskell over the battlefield, he was particularly proud of those mementos, including the silver spurs and a cased photograph of Haskell's Dartmouth graduation portrait. Haskell's horse Dick was killed during the battle. Wert family members said Dick was buried on the Wert farm Wolf's Walk.

J. Howard wrote extensively about the battle of Gettysburg and also gave lectures. He focused on the human toll of the battle, including the children that lost fathers at Gettysburg. Some of the items were personal. The collection even includes a piece of shrapnel that came close to giving J. Howard a grievous wound on Little Round Top during the fighting of the second day.

One item from the Gettysburg field—the field of littered debris—was a Bowie knife. J. Howard recorded he had taken the weapon from the hand of a dead Texan who was killed among the rocks of Devil's Den.

Another set of objects taken from the battlefield elicited great interest from citizens across the country: photographs of family members, especially children, found on the battlefield.

One photograph that J. Howard wrote about showed three children:

> Tightly clasped in the dead soldier's hand was the likeness of three sweet, innocent little children and on them his last gaze had been fastened as, with the one near to soothe his anguish, he had died on the dreary battlefield of slaughter.

J. Howard kept the photographs of children found on the Gettysburg battlefield separate from the other artifacts. They were the innocent victims of the war. They all evoked a certain sadness. While artifacts were placed in trunks and boxes marked with the various names of the battles of Gettysburg, such as Wheatfield, Devil's Den, Round Top, and Rose Farm, the photographs of children were placed in a small mahogany stationary box labeled "Children of the Battlefield."

Attesting to the care of the items collected was D. A. Buehler, who wrote in the preface of J. Howard's *Monuments and Indications of the Gettysburg Battlefield*:

> He was born and raised on the battlefield, he knows every foot of ground, saw every portion of it while the conflict was in progress, and traversed it almost daily for months thereafter, visiting the hospitals, conversing with wounded Union and Confederate actors in the struggle and thereby, familiarizing himself with the incidents of battle. Professor Wert has long been recognized as one of the most brilliant writers [who] brings to his work an ardent sympathy with the cause that triumphed at Gettysburg.

Photographs of the artifacts have been utilized in books, including the 1982 *Time-Life* multi-volume series on the Civil War.

Some of the prized pieces of the collection include a copy of the pass J. Howard received from Washington, DC, in mid-June

Children's photographs that were found on the battlefield.

The eagle head sword of Confederate surgeon Thomas Means of the 10th Georgia.

1863, to raise a colored infantry unit; a gold sword from Thaddeus Stevens; Stevens's eagle walking stick; Gen. John Gibbon's silver medal with his initials; Confederate Gen. Lewis Armistead's stars from the uniform he wore in Pickett's Charge and Armistead's good luck gold coin with an A; Gen. John Geary's sword and mementos; Gen. John Reynolds's military artifacts; Gen. Winfield Scott Hancock's gold embroidered saddle blanket eagle taken from his dead horse after the battle; medical items; weapons; spent ammunition; and J. Howard's own saddle. The medical pannier of a Union surgeon named Rex with original medicines is also in the collection. Rex was at the hospital at the Seminary during the battle of Gettysburg. Union Gen. James Wadsworth's epaulettes were given to J. Howard by Wadsworth's son, a US senator. Gen. Francis Barlow's silver mounted Tiffany saddle that was removed from his dead horse is also part of the collection.

Craig Caba summed up the wide array of unique articles of the Wert collection by listing "major oil paintings, documents, folk art, furniture, battle relics, equipment, and personal mementos from famous people." Memorial collections in the Wert collection, according to Caba, include ones connected with Harriet Beecher Stowe and her son Captain Fred Stowe; John Greenleaf Whittier; William H. Steward; President Abraham Lincoln; Gen. George Gordon Meade; Col. George McFarland of the 151st Pennsylvania;

A highly ornate NCO (non-commissioned officer) sword probably made in the 1850s that was found in the Wheatfield.

Capt. Frederick William Stowe's medicine bottle, pill container, and book on temperance. Stowe was the son of author Harriet Beecher Stowe. He was wounded at Gettysburg. Stowe disappeared in California after the war and was never heard from again.

Fred Stowe's wallet he carried during the war and a brass paperclip Harriet Beecher Stowe used when writing *Uncle Tom's Cabin*.

Gen. Langhorne Wister; Gen. Samuel Crawford; Pennsylvania Governor Andrew Curtin; Lydia Hamilton Smith; David Wills; Edward McPherson; and Thaddeus Stevens.

Some of the individual items Caba cited were Confederate officer Henry Kyd Douglas's silver cased spurs; Gen. Cadmus Wilcox's cased gold spurs; Father William Corby's religious embroidered stole of the Irish Brigade; Gen. Oliver O. Howard's cased binoculars with an inscription to J. Howard, "Compliments of O. O. Howard, Maj. Genl."; Gen. Meade's 5th Corps battle flag, which was abandoned at Meade's headquarters; and Gen. Henry Slokum's miniature saddle bag for orders with an eagle on the front. A letter from Sickles is included in the bag. Col. Strong Vincent's eagle shoulder strap is also a prized possession.

The Wert family collection is much more than artifacts from the battle of Gettysburg. Items relating to politics, religious items, folk art, temperance, public education, and the abolitionist movement in Adams County are included. Four generations of the Wert family contributed to the collection as they took part in fights for freedom in the French and Indian War, American Revolution, the War of 1812, and the Civil War.

The collection contains items from family friends, such as John Greenleaf Whittier and Thaddeus Stevens. When Stevens

A book on the battle of Gettysburg written by J. Howard Wert.

died in 1868, J. Howard received items from the former congressman's office, including a writing table, an armchair, portable desk, file case, and an eagle-carved ivory walking stick. The most unusual item is Stevens's death table that was next to him when he expired.

Items from the Underground Railroad include a rooster-shaped weather vane from his family's barn. The rooster was a symbol of friends to escaped slaves. Other slavery connected items include a punishment ring that was placed around a slave's neck, an anti-slavery token showing a female slave in chains, and a branding iron used to mark runaway slaves returned to captivity. While in the Army J. Howard was in Richmond in the closing days of the Civil War and found a bill of sale for a slave.

Items associated with the 1859 raid by John Brown on the federal arsenal at Harpers Ferry are also included in the collection, including a photograph, pistol, and parts of a noose and gallows.

Family items include an iron trade ax used by the first Jacob Wert, Pennsylvania long rifles fired in the Revolution, and a medallion marking George Washington's presidential inauguration in 1789.

After Professor J. Howard Wert's death in 1920, his son, Howard Houk Wert, took over the collection. Father and son many times walked the battlefield at Gettysburg. Professor Wert wrote in his will that the collection should be kept intact and not divided. The collection has since passed into the hands of Craig Caba, who honors Professor Wert's wishes to keep the collection as one entity.

Chapter Seven

AFTER THE CIVIL WAR

J. Howard never lost contact with those who served during the Civil War. In 1867, he was one of the founders of the Corporal Kelly Post No. 9 of the Grand Army of the Republic (GAR) in Gettysburg and was the post's first chaplain. While in Harrisburg he became associated with GAR Post No. 58.

The same year he helped found Corporal Kelly Post No. 9 of GAR, J. Howard also received a certificate of membership to the Grand Lodge of the Independent Order of Good Templars. The certificate in the Adams County Historical Society is dated June 12, 1867.

He did return to teaching, and immediately after the war was elected principal of Gettysburg High School in 1866. Three years later J. Howard was elected superintendent of Adams County schools. He remained in that position until 1872, when he returned to teach in the schools.

J. Howard was more than qualified to become a teacher. Newly elected Pennsylvania Governor John F. Hartranft wrote a letter dated June 20, 1873, on the letterhead of the Executive Chamber of Harrisburg, certifying J. Howard was in his command at the end of the Civil War and served with credit to himself. The letter stated J. Howard was well qualified to be in the profession of teaching "and is a man worthy of trust." Hartranft

J. Howard Wert's Grand Army of the Republic (GAR) medal.

was a major general in the Civil War and was awarded the Medal of Honor.

J. Howard departed Gettysburg for Harrisburg in 1874 and taught at Boys' High School, where he became first assistant and then principal in 1879. "In that capacity he has made a faithful, painstaking teacher, esteemed by all his former pupils and highly thought of in the community," a Harrisburg paper wrote of him on June 29, 1884. The newspaper article went on to say he wrote for numerous periodicals, including poetry. He also lectured throughout the country.

After fourteen years at Boys' High School, J. Howard became first principal at Harrisburg High School, also known as Central High School. In 1895, he authored *Annals of the Boys' High School of Harrisburg, 1875-1893*. In the book J. Howard details some of his early experiences as a teacher.

J. Howard began by supervising between forty and sixty students in just one room. The subjects he taught were varied, including Latin, Greek, and Roman history. He also taught English history, physical geography, natural history, physiology, government, philosophy, reading, rhetoric, composition, spelling, and declamation. As a principal J. Howard wrote that his classes decreased to seven a week. His workday usually started about 9:00 a.m. and went until 5:00 p.m. J. Howard wrote that he took lunch most days between noon and 2:00 p.m.

At least some of his students revered J. Howard. A Latin class presented J. Howard with a gold pen, holder, and inkstand one year. Another class gave J. Howard a turkey before going off for a break from classes. Another year seniors presented him a box of excellent cigars, but J. Howard noted he had already stopped smoking.

J. Howard continued to champion equal rights during his days in education. He called for fair treatment of minority students and was especially proud, as he wrote in his book on the history of Boys' High School, of three African American students who were admitted, two graduating with honors. The three students peacefully desegregated the school despite fears of violence. One of the students, Reverend William H. Marshall, wrote to J. Howard. According to the book *Harrisburg's Old Eighth Ward*, Marshall's letter said:

> I remember public sentiment did not altogether favor our admission and but for your determination to see that poor and rich, white and black, influential and non-influential, were equal before the law, our years might, nay, would have been much less pleasant.

J. Howard was involved in education for more than three decades. For his work J. Howard was paid between $67.50 and $110.00 per month. For years J. Howard refused to take raises, as he thought teaching was a civic duty. He was fifty-three years old in 1894 when he left the classroom to engage in what he called "literary work."

J. Howard was a prolific writer and contributed hundreds of articles to newspapers and magazines. The exact number is not known. One of his plays was produced in New York City.

J. Howard married Emma Letitia Aughinbaugh of Gettysburg in 1869. She was a teacher. They had four sons—Howard, Edward, Samuel, and Frank—and a daughter Anna. Howard became a postal clerk in Harrisburg; Edward was an attorney in Harrisburg; Samuel was superintendent of the Harrisburg Pike and Pipe Bending Works; Frank was involved in newspapers; and Anna was a Harrisburg supervisor of elementary schools. The family attended Zion Lutheran Church at Fourth and Market Streets, Harrisburg.

A March 1899 article in a New Castle, Pennsylvania, paper detailed J. Howard's literary career:

> Distinguished as he has been as an educator and lecturer, it is as an author that Professor Wert has won his brightest laurels. His exhaustive history of the *Gettysburg Campaign and Monuments*, issues in 1886, is standard authority. His beautiful volume of *Poems of Camp and Hearth*, issued in 1887, should be in the hands of every Grand Army Man,

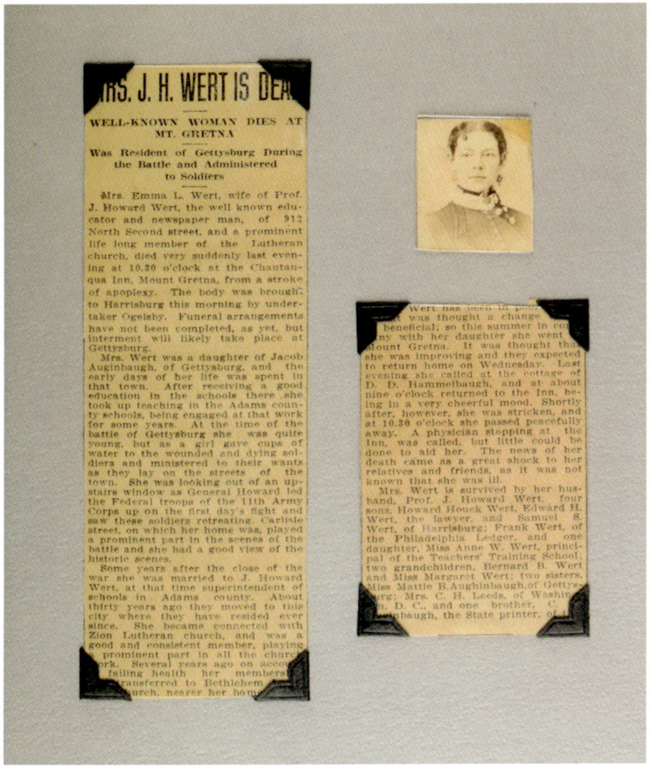

RS. J. H. WERT IS DEA

WELL-KNOWN WOMAN DIES AT MT. GRETNA

Was Resident of Gettysburg During the Battle and Administered to Soldiers

Mrs. Emma L. Wert, wife of Prof. J. Howard Wert, the well known educator and newspaper man, of 912 North Second street, and a prominent life long member of the Lutheran church, died very suddenly last evening at 10.30 o'clock at the Chautauqua Inn, Mount Gretna, from a stroke of apoplexy. The body was brought to Harrisburg this morning by undertaker Ogelsby. Funeral arrangements have not been completed, as yet, but interment will likely take place at Gettysburg.

Mrs. Wert was a daughter of Jacob Auginbaugh, of Gettysburg, and the early days of her life was spent in that town. After receiving a good education in the schools there she took up teaching in the Adams county schools, being engaged at that work for some years. At the time of the battle of Gettysburg she was quite young, but as a girl gave cups of water to the wounded and dying soldiers and ministered to their wants as they lay on the streets of the town. She was looking out of an upstairs window as General Howard led the Federal troops of the 11th Army Corps up on the first day's fight and saw these soldiers retreating. Carlisle street, on which her home was, played a prominent part in the scenes of the battle and she had a good view of the historic scenes.

Some years after the close of the war she was married to J. Howard Wert, at that time superintendent of schools in Adams county. About thirty years ago they moved to this city where they have resided ever since. She became connected with Zion Lutheran church, and was a good and consistent member, playing prominent part in all the churc ork. Several years ago on acco failing health her members ransferred to Bethlehem urch, nearer her hom

Wert has been in poo t was thought a change beneficial; so this summer in co ny with her daughter she went Mount Gretna. It was thought tha she was improving and they expected to return home on Wednesday. Last evening she called at the cottage of D. D. Hammelbaugh, and at about nine o'clock returned to the Inn, being in a very cheerful mood. Shortly after, however, she was stricken, and at 10.30 o'clock she passed peacefully away. A physician stopping at the Inn, was called, but little could be done to aid her. The news of her death came as a great shock to her relatives and friends, as it was not known that she was ill.

Mrs. Wert is survived by her husband, Prof. J. Howard Wert, four sons, Howard Houck Wert, Edward H. Wert, the lawyer, and Samuel S. Wert, of Harrisburg; Frank Wert, of the Philadelphia Ledger, and one daughter, Miss Anne W. Wert, principal of the Teachers' Training School; two grandchildren, Bernard B. Wert and Miss Margaret Wert; two sisters, Miss Mattie B. Aughinbaugh, of Gettysurg; Mrs. C. H. Leeds, of Washin n, D. C., and one brother, C. hbaugh, the State printer, of

A newspaper article on Emma Leiticia Aughinbaugh Wert, wife of J. Howard. As a girl she tended to wounded soldiers during the battle of Gettysburg. She was also a school teacher.

Mrs. Wert's lady GAR medal and mourning cross.

Emma Wert's sewing kit, needles, and other items.

containing as it does, many of the most stirring and thrilling poetical gems yet produced in reference to scenes and incidents of the great conflict. His latest literary work is the weird novel entitled *Alecto and Ebony*, just completed.

In his book *Poems of Camp and Heath* J. Howard wrote:

To the Veterans of the Grand Army of the Republic, Department of Pennsylvania; and especially to my comrades of Post 58, the following of the Great Rebellion are respectfully inscribed by The Author.

J. Howard wrote the first guidebook to the Gettysburg battlefield. His writing credits include: *Two Armies of Gettysburg, Little Stories of Gettysburg, Old Time Notes of Adams County, Gem Souvenir of Gettysburg, In the Hospitals of Gettysburg, Lincoln at Gettysburg*, and *The 50th Anniversary Souvenir Book for the Battle of Gettysburg*. He is credited with writing approximately 400 articles for a variety of publications.

J. Howard is credited with making many reforms in schools in Adams County and Harrisburg. He was a champion of poor immigrants and African-American children completing their education.

While in retirement he lectured at a number of GAR posts in Pennsylvania and throughout New England.

J. Howard also wrote about other historical subjects, including a newspaper article printed in the *Harrisburg Telegraph* on October 21, 1904, about "The Fremont Campaign of 1856: First Presidential Struggle of the Republican Party." The Wert collection contains a number of presidential memorabilia.

The headline highlighted the John C. Fremont campaign, but the article was a review of presidential campaigns for almost two decades. J. Howard's knowledge of presidential history became the fabric of the newspaper article. He recounted changes in the way campaigns were conducted over the years, including having mass rallies where thousands of people gathered from hundreds of miles to hear campaign speeches and sing campaign songs. He also noted that large numbers of the "fair sex" began attending.

The first campaign J. Howard wrote about remembering personally, even though he was a young boy, was the 1844 contest between Henry Clay and James Polk. By J. Howard's writing he seemed to be a fan of Clay and relayed information from a Harrisburg resident who said during Clay's parade in the city there were two highly unusual sights: a canal boat on wheels and an enormous stuffed ox on a float—no less unusual—with butcher Thomas Osler.

His favorite presidential candidates of the time did not win at the polls. J. Howard called the 1848 Democratic candidate Lewis Cass one of the "purest and noblest statesman this country has produced." However, Whig candidate Zachary Taylor won the election. J. Howard pointed out Taylor's success as a military officer in the war with Mexico carried the election. Taylor did not complete his term in office, as he died July 8, 1850, from what some believe was poisoning from tainted food served at an event at the Washington Monument. Vice President Millard Fillmore completed Taylor's term of office.

While J. Howard may have somewhat recalled the 1844 election, he wrote that during the 1852 campaign he became a participant by frequently attending night meetings during the three months preceding the election. The election again ended in defeat for a favored candidate, Winfield Scott. J. Howard wrote, "Never was a campaign more heroically fought. Never did a candidate go down to a more crushing defeat than Winfield Scott."

Scott, running as a Whig candidate, won only four states against Democrat Franklin Pierce. According to J. Howard's commentary:

> And the bitterness of the defeat was that the greatest soldier of the generation met his Waterloo at the hands of a man, scarcely known outside of New Hampshire previous to his nomination, which had been, for a short time, a subaltern under Scott in Mexico without gaining any special distinction.

Luther W. Minnigh was a friend of J. Howard Wert and signed a book used at the Gettysburg Address. Minnigh is shown in a photograph of guides at Gettysburg on Little Round Top. Minnigh authored *Gettysburg: What They Did Here*.

Adam Wert certainly encouraged his son to get involved in politics, and since the Whig party was known for anti-slavery stances the Wert family usually backed those candidates. J. Howard remembered large Whig gatherings in Niagara Falls and Harrisburg and wondered if any of the newspaper readers in 1904 recalled the events. J. Howard also quoted from a story of the September 24, 1852, edition of the *Gettysburg Star* newspaper, where Whigs were characterized as a "low, mean, dirty, sneaking, stinking Raccoon party, which not only looks bad, but smells bad."

The campaign, according to J. Howard, saw the deaths of two of the leading members of the Whig party: Henry Clay and Daniel Webster. Those deaths, J. Howard wrote, foretold the demise of the Whigs.

Indeed, by the time of the next presidential election the Whig party was gone and two new parties were formed: the Republicans and Americans, known as the Know Nothings. John C. Fremont was the Republican candidate, former President Millard Fillmore represented the Know Nothings, and Pennsylvanian James Buchanan was the Democratic candidate, defeating President

Pierce. The Republicans were staunchly anti-slavery and favored by the Wert family.

The wonderful campaign of 1856, as Wert called the election, almost elevated John C. Fremont to the presidency. The slavery issue was at the center of the campaign, with Buchanan warning the country that a Republican victory would lead the country into civil war. The Republican party was fighting legislation that would lead to the spread of slavery throughout the country.

Fremont was the perfect candidate for the Republican party, as he was a dashing army officer, and many of the Republican members were young men from northern states. For the three months before the election politics overshadowed commerce and filled most of the newspaper space, according to J. Howard. "It was politics everywhere; and, often, politics of not a very peaceable character," he wrote.

On the surface J. Howard wrote: "The campaigns were a whirlwind of hurrah with monster mass meetings with miles of torches. Beneath the surface the campaigns were structured and organized with meetings in virtually every school, crossroad and tavern." Newspapers joined the fray with editorials and stories.

In J. Howard's home county of Adams, the Republican party started to organize late in the campaign. In May 1856, the little village of New Oxford began to gather support for the Republicans, and then in late August, the *Gettysburg Star* became pro-Republican. Republican meetings in Gettysburg and Hanover—towns close to the Mason-Dixon Line—were threatened with violence, but the meetings were held. Wert reported some fighting and shooting between Republicans and Democratic supporters. A few meetings were held south of the line in Maryland.

J. Howard recounted the bloody fighting in Kansas over slavery and the attack on Senator Charles Sumner of Massachusetts by Representative Preston Brooks of South Carolina. Several days after Sumner delivered a strident speech against those sacking Kansas and also South Carolina Senator Andrew Butler, Brooks entered the Senate and beat Sumner with a gold-tipped cane, breaking the weapon. Brooks was fined $300 and went home.

Buchanan became president of the United States and J. Howard believed he was in an almost impossible position. J. Howard wrote, "James Buchanan, pure and dignified in all the relations of life, private and public, reached the presidency, the goal of his life's aspirations, only to find it a heritage of trouble."

Col. A. K. McClure of Chambersburg was an editor, United States Marshal, member of the Pennsylvania House of Representatives and Senate, and a historian. He was active in the Republican Party in Pennsylvania. He received an advance copy of J. Howard's article "The Fremont Campaign of 1856: First Presidential Struggle of the Republican Party." McClure wrote of the article: "It is presented with rare accuracy, and the abiding interest of the struggle is kept up from beginning to end. I am glad, indeed, that you have furnished this chapter to the political history of the country relating to a period that is not now well understood."

Besides history, poetry was one of J. Howard's loves. One report noted J. Howard could recall more than 60,000 lines of poetry, some American and some English.

J. Howard wrote about the Eighth Ward of Harrisburg in a series of thirty-five articles in the *Harrisburg Patriot*, beginning November 18, 1912. J. Howard described the people who lived in that section of Harrisburg—both the good and the bad—and community life. While he described the politics of the ward, J. Howard also devoted space to the many churches of his community and the businesses that employed residents in a number of manufacturing concerns. J. Howard spent equal time writing of the gangs, vice, orgies, and speakeasies of the ward.

His final home was a row house near the intersection of North Second and Forster Streets, Harrisburg. He died on the evening of March 11, 1920, at age eighty after a long illness. His body was taken by train to Gettysburg, where it was met by his sons and Civil War comrades. He was buried in the town's Evergreen Cemetery. J. Howard Wert's obituary noted:

> PROFESSOR WERT, LONG ILL, DIES
> Former Head of County Schools Was Well Known Writer.

WROTE SEVERAL NOVELS

Took Part in Civil War Playing a Part in the Battle of Gettysburg. Wrote History of Conflict.

Professor J. Howard Wert, well known writer and educator, with many friends in Adams County where he was the superintendent of schools for several years, died Thursday night at his home in Harrisburg after a long illness at an advanced age. He had been seriously ill for some weeks and his death was not unexpected. For years he had been living retired.

Professor J. Howard Wert was born on a farm near Gettysburg, the only child of Adam and Catherine (Houghtelin) Wert. His father, a man of exceptional ability, was a leader among Pennsylvania Abolitionists. His mother, also very gifted, was very conspicuous in the annals of early Methodism in Southern Pennsylvania.

After a preliminary course in the rural public schools and the Gettysburg High School, in all of which he evinced a precocity which made him the marvel of the community, the deceased spent six years at Gettysburg College, graduating in 1861.

While in college, he acquired considerable reputation as a writer; becoming a contributor to nearly all the Boston and New York literary periodicals of that day.

His first serial, "The Mystic League of Three," a novel in twenty chapters, written while in the Sophomore year, won a prize and was published in Frank Queen's "New York Clipper." Having been dramatized, it was produced soon after at one of the Bowery theaters, with a run of 4 consecutive nights. It was a story of sporting life in the large cities written at a time that the young author had never seen a larger town than Gettysburg.

In various capacities, Professor Wert saw many of the stirring scenes of the Civil War, including the battle of Gettysburg, where he had exceptional opportunities for

observation both during and after the conflict. During the Gettysburg campaign he did considerable service as a scout for which he was well fitted by his intimate knowledge of the whole surrounding country. On the afternoon of the first day of the battle, he was the guide who conducted the head of General Slocum's 12th Corps to the position it subsequently held in Culp's Hill, after having informed the officers leading the column of the positions which Early's Confederate Corps had gained on the other side of Rock Creek.

Concerning the decisive battle he had written many valuable articles and pamphlets, as well as an extended history, first published in 1886, which had sold extensively on trains and on the field for several years. A second Gettysburg battle history written for a New York syndicate as a souvenir gift to G.A.R. posts in connection with the Semi-Centennial celebration of 1913, and published from the plant of the *Harrisburg Telegraph* was characterized by a competent reviewer as "The most vivid pen-portraiture of the great battle ever written, and one of the finest specimens of historic word painting in the English language."

The close of the war found Professor Wert a lieutenant in Company G, 209th Pennsylvania Volunteers. This regiment served first in Butler's Army of the James, and then became a part of Hartranft's celebrated Pennsylvania command, — the Third Division, Ninth Army Corps, Army of the Potomac. With it the deceased participated in some of the severest engagements around Richmond and Petersburg including the storming of the latter city; and followed up Lee's retreating army to the surrender at Appomattox.

He also participated in the Grand Review of the Army of the Potomac, May 23, 1865, when, for seven continuous hours, 80,000 veterans, solidly massed from curb to curb, swept down Pennsylvania Avenue, at the nation's capital, passing before President of the United States and General Grant.

Chapter Eight

RARITIES OF GETTYSBURG

J. Howard dedicated the years after the Civil War to educating the public about the participants of Gettysburg and preserving the historic artifacts of the pivotal battle of the Civil War. He spent many hours giving public talks on the subject of Gettysburg and interacting with the participants of the struggle in the small town in Adams County, Pennsylvania.

Educating the public was one of J. Howard's goals. He utilized many of the rare items from his collection to illustrate his talks. To his trained eye, J. Howard could identify the type of weapon used by soldiers during the battle, and also tell where Confederates made modifications to modernize their weapons to keep them in working order. J. Howard's expertise was passed down to future generations, along with his J. Howard Wert Gettysburg Collection™.

J. Howard and his collection received national recognition during his lifetime. D. A. Buehler of the Gettysburg Battlefield Memorial Association wrote about J. Howard's pedigree as a collector: "Born and raised on the battlefield (J. Howard) knows every foot of ground, saw every portion of it while the conflict was in progress and traversed it almost daily for months thereafter, visiting the hospitals, conversing with wounded Union and Confederate soldiers in the struggle and thereby familiarizing himself with the incidents of the battle."

In August 1888, *Frank Leslie's Popular Monthly* called him an eyewitness to history. In 1910, the *New York Herald* proclaimed the Wert collection of relics from Gettysburg could not be duplicated in any museum in the country, and many of the items are seldom found in similar collections.

The collection's fame carried on after J. Howard's death. The Baltimore Evening Sun wrote an article about the 1963 exhibit at the Shriver Homestead at Union Mills as part of a Gettysburg centennial exhibit. The article noted many of the items exhibited had not been seen since the Civil War. J. Howard was also lauded in a *Time-Life* Gettysburg publication in 1984. Historian Brian C. Pohanka wrote that, "J. Howard returned often to the ravaged field, selecting and carefully identifying items from the debris with a keen eye for the memorable and poignant."

J. Howard's mission of education continues today, as curator Craig Caba has been to many sections of the United States displaying the Wert collection. The collection has been consulted by historians and authors for research. Artifacts, such as the podium used by President Abraham Lincoln for his Gettysburg Address, have been loaned to various cultural and historical organizations (The podium was been shown in the Union League in Philadelphia). A number of items from the collection were featured at the 150th anniversary celebration of the City of Harrisburg, the National Civil War Medical Museum, and at Antietam National Park. Craig has given programs at many Civil War Round Table meetings.

Relics found from the Third Corps after fighting on July 2, 1863, including a Savage pistol, non-commissioned officer's belt buckle, officer's sword knot, Lady Liberty CDV, and a maple drum stick, along with coins and a purse.

Top: A Richmond rifle that was damaged and had the barrel cut down and a Fayetteville lock added. The hybrid carbine was made in the Confederacy and found at Hunterstown on July 2, where a cavalry fight took place as part of the Gettysburg campaign. Bottom: An English Enfield carbine used by C. Howza of Cobb's Legion during a cavalry battle at Hunterstown on July 2, 1863.

Confederate flintlock converted to percussion during the early part of the Civil War. The weapon was owned by Charles Neuffer of Company A, 2nd South Carolina of Kershaw's Brigade. Neuffer died of wounds he received at Gettysburg.

A Harper's Ferry half-stock rifle from the early 1800s with a Confederate percussion conversion. The weapon was used by a sharpshooter and recovered on Culp's Hill.

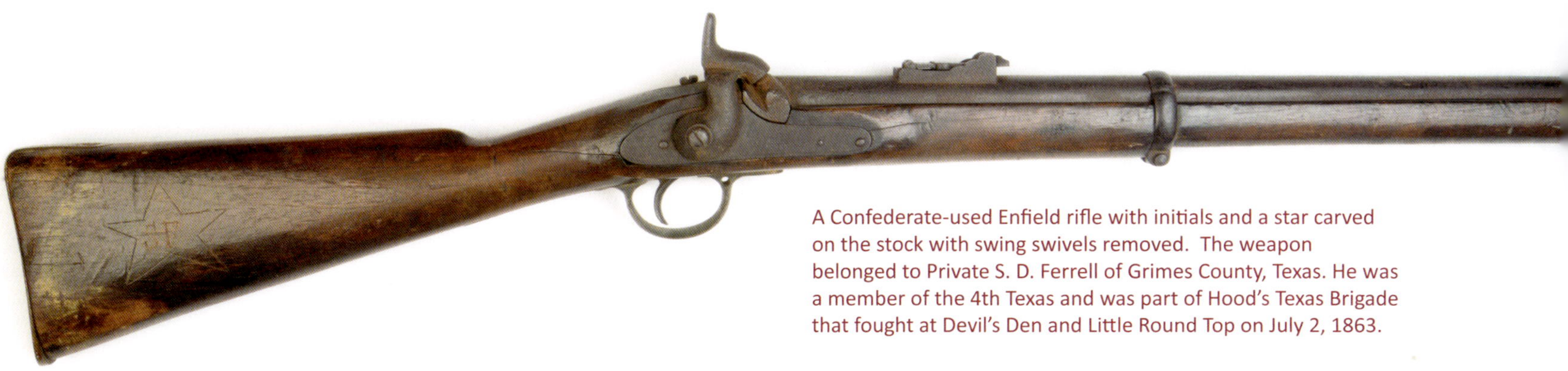

A Confederate-used Enfield rifle with initials and a star carved on the stock with swing swivels removed. The weapon belonged to Private S. D. Ferrell of Grimes County, Texas. He was a member of the 4th Texas and was part of Hood's Texas Brigade that fought at Devil's Den and Little Round Top on July 2, 1863.

Top: The rifle was made in St. Louis and has a distinctive patch box made by Renaud Beauvais, a St. Louis-based gunsmith. J. Howard picked up the weapon used by a member of the 3rd Arkansas among the rocks at Devil's Den. Bottom: A Confederate-used Mississippi rifle with a replaced Confederate rear site. The weapon had the initials W. D. and belonged to William Dancey of the 47th North Carolina.

An all hand-forged iron sharpshooter rifle found near the body of a Rebel in John Rupp's tannery.

A percussion musket converted with a distinctive hammer. The weapon carried an 1812 mark and was carried by James W. Duke of Company C, 17th Mississippi.

Sword carried by Gen. John Reynolds of Pennsylvania. Reynolds was killed during the first day of fighting. The sword was placed on his coffin.

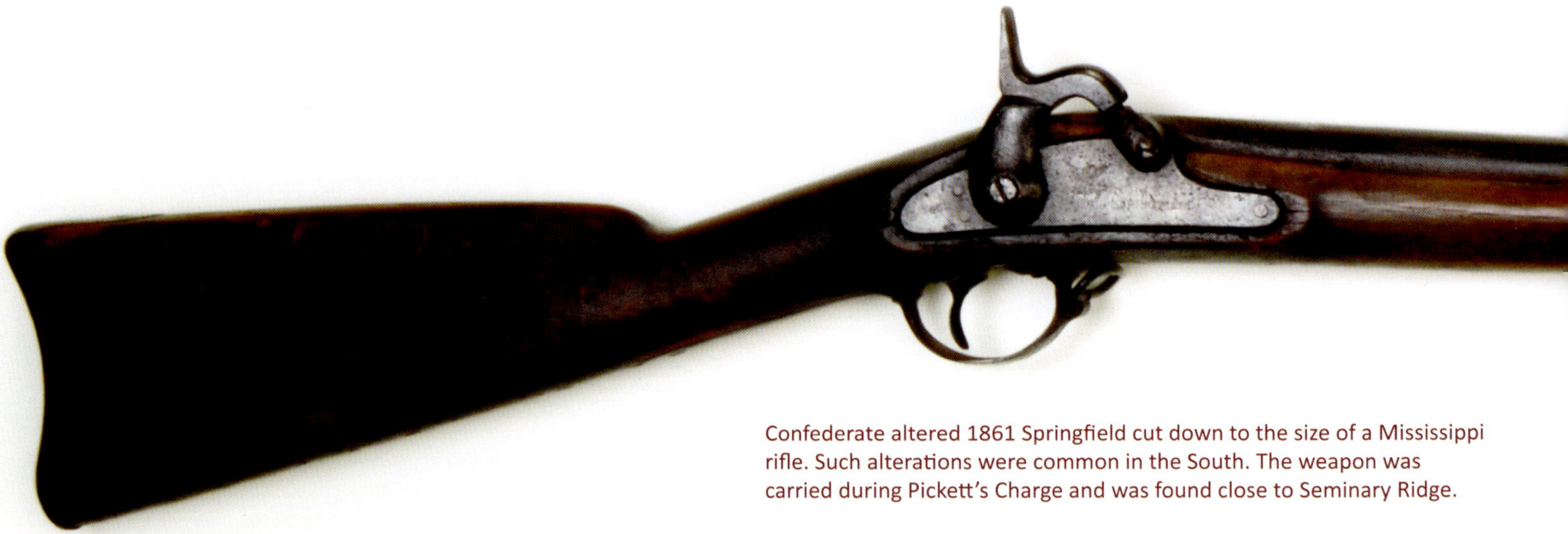

Confederate altered 1861 Springfield cut down to the size of a Mississippi rifle. Such alterations were common in the South. The weapon was carried during Pickett's Charge and was found close to Seminary Ridge.

A Confederate-used 1827 cavalry musketoon made from a captured musket. The weapon had the initials J. R. E. on it and belonged to James Ellison of Louisiana, a member of Madison Light Artillery, part of Alexander's artillery.

A Confederate musket converted from flint lock to percussion by the use of a hand-forged hammer found in the Wheatfield. The weapon had a W on the stock.

A Maryland marked militia musket converted to percussion and found on Culp's Hill, where Confederate Maryland troops fought.

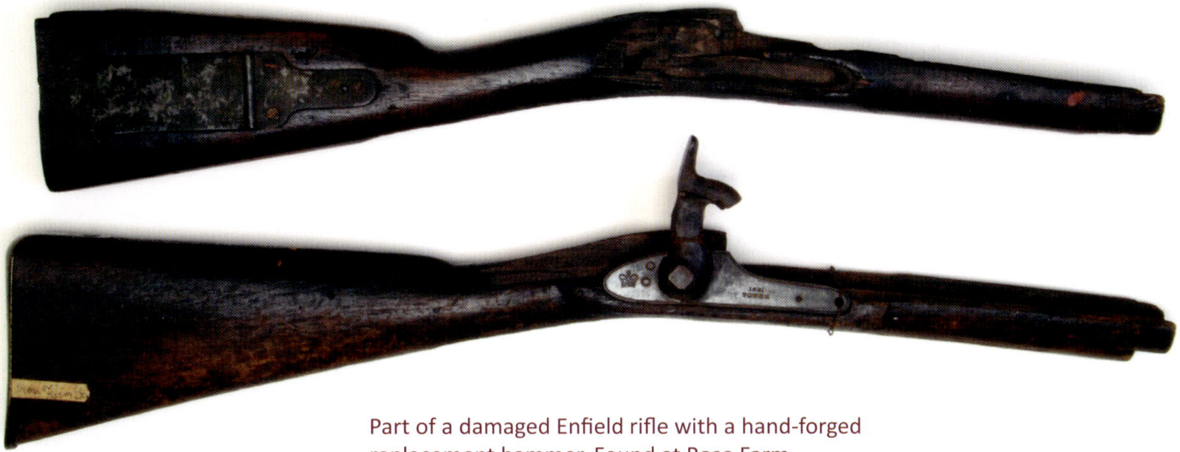

Part of a damaged Enfield rifle with a hand-forged replacement hammer. Found at Rose Farm.

J. Howard Wert campaign hat and dust brush.

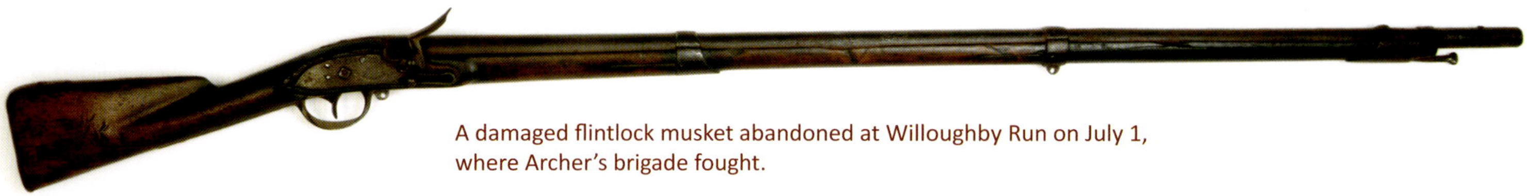

A damaged flintlock musket abandoned at Willoughby Run on July 1, where Archer's brigade fought.

An 1863 Richmond rifled musket used during Pickett's Charge found near the Emmitsburg Road.

A rare imported British Brunswick sharpshooter rifle captured July 1, 1863, at the Railroad Cut. The Confederate soldier broke the stock as an act of defiance after surrendering.

APPENDIX A

J. HOWARD WERT'S POETRY

J. Howard Wert loved poetry and gathered and published a book of poems, *Poems of Camp and Hearth*, in 1887. The book included poems about Gettysburg.

I - Under the Oaks of Rock Creek.
Culp's Hill: 1853-1863-1883
Under the oaks of Rock Creek,
Two blithesome boys were straying,
And by each loaded shell-bark tree
Their laggard steps delaying:
Above, the rock-strewn hill-top towered,
In peaceful silence dreaming;
And through the autumn-colored woods
A mellow light was streaming.

Under the oaks of Rock Creek –
Five years have passed away;
Again, through gorgeous tree-tops,
Shone autumn's placid ray.
The *one* is there to manhood grown,
"Lenore" is by his side;
For both had loved one maiden fair,
But she'll be the Southron's bride.

Under the oaks of Rock Creek,
Again five years have passed:
Along the tiny, sluggish stream
Ten thousand men are massed;
Grim Ewell rode the lines along
Of veterans clad in gray,
And `gainst the frowning, rock peak
The charging masses sway.

Under the oaks of Rock Creek
Flashed miles of sheet flame;
Right at the works a captain fell
Before the deadly aim
Of one, who wore the Federal blue,
In death the dead besides;
From out the gaping bullet wound
Danced quick life's ebbing tide.

Under the oaks of Rock Creek,
In trenches long and deep,
The swollen courses of the gray
Are laid in dreamless sleep.
"With tears by boyhood's memories stirred,
In death a foe no more,
I place thee `neath the oaks where erst
You won your wife `Lenore!`"

Under the oaks of Rock Creek,
When twenty years had fled,
A woman walked, with pensive step,
Those acres of the dead.
Dead are the giant oak trees,
Life shot from every pore;
And they are crumbling into dust
Like the heat of the lone "Lenore."

II – BROWN'S BATTERY B

Around the clump, world-storied spot –
Rebellion's highest wave,
When Webb, and Hall, and Harrow fought,
And dug secession's grave,
Stand thickly-clustered, granite piles,
But none more dear to me,
O'er all those history-breathing miles,
Than that of battery B

A humble, modest shaft, 'tis true,
But marks where heroes stood,
No braver ever wore the blue,
Or poured life's precious flood.
Hosannas raise and thanks to God,
Who kept our nation free;
And, 'mongst the men who drenched this sod,
Remember battery B

Two days they faced the sulphurous wave
Of grape and shot and shell;
Where Humphreys' muskets answer gave
To the Georgian battle yell;
Where Pickett's men with valor fought,
In hopes of victory,
But fell in swaths beneath the shot
From gallant battery B

Above the deadliest carnage rose
Brown's words of stern command,
Until he fell in mortal throes,
Fighting to save our land;
And through of all Rhode Island's sons,
Remained not one in three,
Yet still they served the smoking guns
Of fearless battery B

Aye, love fore'er those soldiers brave,
Who sleep beneath the sod;
Freely for us their lives they gave;
None braver ever trod
The smoke-wreathed field of grim-faced death.
That flowed in crimson sea.
Entwined with glory's greenest wreath
Is the roll of battery B.

III – THE EXCELSIOR BRIGADE

A brilliant mile of serried steel,
Beneath the shining sun;
In line the gallant veterans wheel –
The work of death's begun;
A solid mile of silvery steel,
A solid mile of blue:
Ah! Many a Southern foe shall feel
Their bullets quick and true.

It is the gallant army corps,
The gallant Sickles led,
That in Virginia oft before
For the starry banner bled:
Now once again to the pealing sound
Of bugles and of drums,
They march on Pennsylvania ground,
To fight for Northern homes.

No grander sight was ever spread
'Neath July's burning ray,
Than the diamonded host, the martial tread,
On its advancing way;
No ghastlier sight was ever seen
On fields of carnage wild
Than the smoking lines, and all between
With bloody courses piled:

For Longstreet's veteran legions charge
In stern and swift array;
O never rolled so fierce, so large.
The sweep of the storied gray
And Hill's battalions tried and true
Join in the lurid fray,
And Barksdale carves, through lines of blue,
The Mississippians' way

From Sherfy's orchard east and west
The heated batteries play;
On round Top's blood-besprinkled crest
The fighting masses sway;
The Wheat-field is a pool of blood,
Before the shut of day,
Where Birney struggles, 'mid the flood,
To hold the fox at bay:

Along the line of Humphreys' fell
The deadly leaden rain,
With whiz of grape and shriek of shell,
And sickening cries of pain.
No heroes braver held their place
'Mid the horrors of the fight;
And fronted death, face pressed to face,
Till the veil of pitying night

Had the field and the dead it bore,
Than the soldiers brave and grand,
Whose banners flapped "EXCELSIOR,"
As the name of the command;
And none more bravely, grandly fought,
'Mid that echoing fire of hell.
With woe was the deadly answer fraught
They gave the Southern yell.

Ah! Many a widow in her weeds
Will sadly mourn for aye,
The Excelsior boys and their valiant deeds
On that fierce-fought battle-day.
Through their glad be torn to a single shred,
And shot from its resting place,
And piled beneath it the mangled dead,
It has never known disgrace.

A shattered mile of blood-dimmed steel,
Beneath the setting sun;
O'er wounded comrades now they kneel,
The work of death is done.
One half of all that gallant corps
Of the diamond and the blue,
With life or wounds, that dark field o'ver,
Have sealed devotion true.

But as the thrilling cheers arise
From those who yet remain,
Be-echoed to the vaulting skies
From the dreary battle-plain;
The thinned EXCELSIORS still maintain
Their banner in its place,
For, 'mid the deadliest leaden rain,
It will never know disgrace.

APPENDIX B

PARTIAL LIST OF BOOKS BY J. HOWARD WERT

A Complete Hand-book of the Monuments and Indications and Guide to the Positions on the Gettysburg Battlefield

The Two Great Armies at Gettysburg, Being Chapters I, II and III of Gettysburg and Its Monuments

Poems of Camp and Hearth

Little Stories of Gettysburg

Historical Souvenir of the Fiftieth Anniversary of the Battle of Gettysburg, July 1–4, 1913

In the Hospitals of Gettysburg

Gettysburg Gem Souvenir

History of the 209th Regiment, Pennsylvania Volunteer Infantry

Annals of the Boy's High School of Harrisburg 1875-1893

Mystic League of Three (novel)

God's Centennial

Rhyme and Reason

Alecto and Ebony (novel)

Five Years in the Grave

School Composition Work Made Attractive

The Battle of Gettysburg an Historical Account

Gettysburg, Pennsylvania Railroad

Two Armies at Gettysburg

BIBLIOGRAPHY

Barton, Michael, and Jessica Dorman. *Harrisburg's Old Eighth Ward.* Charleston, SC: Arcadia Publishing, 2002.

Bates, Samuel P. *History of the Pennsylvania Volunteers, 1861-65.* Harrisburg: Harrisburg Legislature, B. Singerly, State Printer, 1868.

Caba, G. Craig. *Gettysburg 1836 Battle Over Slavery.* Gettysburg: G. Craig Caba Antiques and Publishers, 1997.

Caba, G. Craig, and Amanda Fenstermacher. *Lost Children of the Battlefield: A Collection of Photographs Found at Gettysburg.* Enola: G. Craig Caba Antiques and Publishers, 2004.

Caba, G. Craig. *Riding With Frank: Observations of Lieutenant Frank Haskell and J. Howard Wert After the Battle of Gettysburg, July 6, 1863*. Enola: G. Craig Caba Antiques and Publishers, 2013.

Cramer, Zadok. *The Navigator: Containing Directions for Navigating the Monongahela, Allegheny, Ohio and Mississippi*. Pittsburgh: Cramer, Spear & Echbaum, 1811.

Harrisburg Telegraph. *Wert, Historian, Late Lt. Penna Volunteers.* Harrisburg: Harrisburg Telegraph, 1913.

Holzer, Harold. *Lincoln and the Power of the Press.* New York: Simon and Schuster, 2014

Lincoln Group of District of Columbia. *Day By Day.* http://www.lincolngroup.org/.

New Castle News. Newspaper article. New Castle: *New Castle News*, March 1889.

Swift, Robert. *The J. Howard Wert Collection*. Gettysburg: Gettysburg Magazine, Issue 38 p. 114-117.

Wert, J. Howard. *Camp and Hearth*. Harrisburg: Harrisburg Publishing Company, 1897.

Wert, J. Howard. *Episodes of Gettysburg and the Underground Railroad as witnessed and recorded by Professor J. Howard Wert*. Gettysburg: G. Craig Caba Antiques, 1998.

Wert, J. Howard. *Historical Souvenir of the Fiftieth Anniversary of the Battle of Gettysburg*. Harrisburg: *Harrisburg Telegraph*, 1913.

INDEX